TREATISE
ORCHID
su wen chapter 8

MONKEY PRESS

Monkey Press is named after the Monkey King in The Journey to the West, the 16th century classical novel by Wu Chengen. Monkey blends skill, initiative and wisdom with the spirit of freedom, irreverence and a touch of mischief.

CHINESE MEDICINE FROM THE CLASSICS
Also in the same series:

The Lung
The Kidneys
Spleen and Stomach
The Heart in Ling Shu Chapter 8
Heart Master, Triple Heater
The Liver
The Way of Heaven: Su Wen Chapters 1 and 2
The Seven Emotions
The Eight Extraordinary Meridians
Essence, Spirit, Blood and Qi
The Extraordinary Fu

THE SECRET TREATISE OF THE SPIRITUAL ORCHID
Nei jing Su wen chapter 8

Claude Larre
Elisabeth Rochat de la Vallée

MONKEY PRESS

Published by
MONKEY PRESS

© Monkey Press 2003 First edition 1987

CHINESE MEDICINE FROM THE CLASSICS:
The Secret Treatise of the Spiritual Orchid
Claude Larre and Elisabeth Rochat de la Vallée

www.monkeypress.net

All rights reserved. No part of this book may be reproduced in any form without written permission from the publisher.

ISBN 1 872468 00 4

Text editor: Caroline Root
Production and design: Sandra Hill
Calligraphy: Qu Lei Lei

Cover design: Mark Jacobs
Printed by Spider Web, London

CONTENTS

Foreword by Peter Eckman
Preface to the revised edition
Introduction   1
The first chapters of the Su wen   7

Suwen chapter 8:   23
The heart, *xin* 心   36
The lung, *fei* 肺   49
The liver, *gan* 肝   58
The gallbladder, *dan* 膽   73
Tan zhong 膻中   90
The spleen and stomach, *pi wei* 脾胃   109
The large intestine, *da chang* 大腸   115
The small intestine, *xiao chang* 小腸   119
The kidneys, *shen* 腎   132
The triple heater, *san jiao* 三焦   142
The bladder, *pang guang* 膀胱   146

Conclusion   154

Appendix   165
Su wen chapter 8: Translation of the text
Chinese text (characters 1-163)
Index   171

FOREWORD

I first encountered Father Claude Larre in May of 1983 at the annual conference of the Traditional Acupuncture Foundation in the Shoreham Hotel in Washington, D.C. As I am the goat in this story, I can only excuse myself as having been overwhelmed by the allure of my fellow speakers among whom were Manfred Porkert, Fritjof Capra, Yeshi Donden, Ted Kaptchuk, Yves Requena and Claude Larre - quite a line-up! I remember when Father Larre got on stage to give his short proselytizing speech on Sinology for Acupuncturists all I could think of was, 'Who does this Larre think he is? There's no way I (or anyone else here) is about to start learning to read Chinese.' After all, I'd been to medical school, and I knew all about memorizing more bits of information than I could ever hope to retain. I couldn't wait for this soft-spoken and eccentric priest to be finished so I could immerse myself in the presentations of the other illustrious speakers, and I more or less dismissed him from my mind (or so I thought).

But something in his speech had stuck with me, in spite of myself. I went out and bought his recommended text, Wieger's Chinese Characters and if there's one thing I'm a sucker for, it's a good book. Lo and behold, four months later, I found myself in England studying the Chinese text of the Su wen with Father Larre, this time with Julia Measures, Roger Hill, Caroline Root and Peter Firebrace as classmates! Claude Larre has this kind of effect on people, planting seeds that often aren't even noticed at first, but which nonetheless take root at a deep level and produce a decidedly strong growth.

Having begun to study with Father Larre, I subsequently accompanied him on a trip to China and later participated with him in a collaborative teaching project that gave me a taste of what you can experience reading these transcripts of him work with Elisabeth Rochat de la Vallée. These two provide the best example of tandem teaching I can recall - Larre with his years of living in China and becoming Chinese in his mind, and Rochat with her fastidious study of the classical Chinese texts, are a once in a lifetime resource. Through the work they have done under the auspices of the European School of Acupuncture, numerous practitioners such as myself have been given a new appreciation of the classics.

One does not have to be an expert sinologist to benefit from the studies they encourage - the results begin to show almost immediately, and grow proportionately to the effort invested. All of the Larre/Rochat publications put out by Monkey Press are well worth careful study, and for the beginner in sinology, I cannot recommend highly enough attending at least one class with these two teachers who are continuing to instruct both newcomers and advanced students in Europe and the U.S. In The Secret Treatise of the Spiritual Orchid you have perhaps the most refined example of their teaching. I hope after reading it, the same seed will be planted in you as in me.

Peter Eckman, MD, PhD, MAc (UK)
Goat Hill House, San Francisco, 1992

PREFACE TO THE THIRD EDITION

This new edition of The Secret Treatise of the Spiritual Orchid appears just over ten years after the second was published in 1992. During that time the study, practice and in fact the whole profession of Chinese Medicine has evolved and matured in a wonderfully positive way. It seems appropriate therefore to acknowledge the prescience and vision of Peter Firebrace in his initiation of the series of seminars given by Father Claude Larre and Elisabeth Rochat de la Vallée which began in London in 1985. From that beginning there followed a whole series of seminars, along with their transcripts which have been published by Monkey Press. That these are now used as text books for students bears witness to their perennial wisdom.

It is also necessary to honour the memory of Father Larre, who died in December 2001. For those fortunate enough to know and study with him, his inspiration and example were extraordinary and profound. For those who find his spirit through the words reproduced in the Monkey Press books and his other writings, let his vast learning, original interpretations and mischievous humour speak to and resonate within you. A deceptively simple sentence will often reveal many layers of meaning and may surprise you with its insight.

Father Larre died soon after the completion of the magnificent Ricci Dictionary which had been an ongoing project for himself and Elisabeth for over 20 years. This awe-inspiring rendering of every Chinese character and associated groups of characters into French is a testament to Father Larre's firm belief in the necessity of students and practitioners using and understanding Chinese characters in order to make sense of the ancient texts of Chinese medicine and philosophy. For this reason, The Secret Treatise of the Spiritual Orchid contains many references to Dr. L. Wieger's 'Chinese Characters', published by Dover Books, which is an invaluable book on the etymology, history and meaning of Chinese characters. Father Larre considered it to be a fundamental source book for students of Chinese medicine.

In reading this book it is important to remember that neither of the speakers have English as their first language. Although the text has been edited, much has been left just as it was spoken. Hence some terminology is perhaps a little unfamiliar for today's students and practitioners, and the use of the male and female pronouns occasionally closer to their usage in French than in current English. It would be a shame to let these usages detract from the overall meaning and significance of the text. As Peter Firebrace wrote in his preface to the 1992 edition: 'Su wen chapter 8 is a text of simplicity and clarity, of deceptive brevity that hides a wealth of potent images. It is a keynote chapter sketching a Confucian-style hierarchy and functioning as each organ character is introduced in turn. As an overview of the *zangfu* it is hard to beat'.

Caroline Root July 2003

The Secret Treatise of the Spiritual Orchid, *ling lan mi dian lun*

INTRODUCTION

Claude Larre: Before introducing the text, I would like to say a few words about our backround and the European School of Acupuncture. The founder was Doctor Jean Schatz, an outstanding character. He was trained first in Occidental medicine, and then lived in Algeria, where he turned to acupuncture. Due to personal circumstances he came back to France and established himself with his family in Paris. I remember one bright Sunday at some friends' house when he was explaining the *dao* (道). I was baffled to see a man without any knowledge of Daoism speaking about how things are in the name of the *dao* itself. Shyly I raised my finger: 'If I am permitted, I would ask the Doctor to re-examine the subject, because I am lost in all these explanations, and there is nothing of what you speak in Daoism as far as I know.'

One year later he asked me whether I would join him in the venture of creating a school where Chinese texts would be the basis of the teaching. I said that I was not ready to help with that since I did now know Chinese medical, or so-called, medical texts. If it had been limited to Lao zi (the Dao de jing), or Zhuang zi, or to the other outstanding works in the classical literature I would have joined him, but I felt this was not possible. At that time Elisabeth Rochat de la Vallée had already been working with me for five years, and was herself ready to enter this venture. We started learning the classics at night with a group of four, five or six people. Nowadays I would be very ashamed of the translations we were doing at that time. I feel they have been improving since then, but another stretch of time will be needed to really master what is inside the classical texts.

The fact is that the way the Chinese express themselves is conveyed to us through means which are very far from our alphabetic languages in the Occident. The problem is that the feeling the Chinese have when contemplating nature working outside or inside themselves, although genuine to them is awkward for most of us. The question is not whether this term meridian or acupuncture point is right or not, this is just a convention. Meridian is the English expression for something which has never been thought of by the Chinese as a meridian. The same goes for points and organs and all the rest. The problem is that thousands and thousands of Chinese characters and expressions are not grounded in our minds as they are in the Chinese mind. Notwithstanding the differences of appreciation the Chinese may have from one text to another, from one author to another, or from one main text to a commentator, they all belong to the same family of minds. But the differences we find in English or French textbooks are not reconcilable. On the contrary, differences of views expressed in Western textbooks of Chinese medicine are just irreconcilable contradictions, if not pure nonsense. They stem from the imagination of people of different origins not sharing the same approach to life. If it is not necessary to know what *qi* is, it is at least necessary to be conscious of one's own life.

Whenever we find an acupuncturist, whether a student, practitioner or teacher, who knows through bodily consciousness, that he or she is a permanent product of the universe, and has the feeling of something on the move, he needs a word for expressing this, and the word is *qi* (氣). But he also has to know where to store this *qi*, how to use it, and how to replace it. For this he needs more vocabulary. He knows that he is mortal, that his life comes from somewhere, goes through him, and continues somewhere after him. For all these circumstances he needs to find words which are not disconnected from the unity of life. Everywhere we now hear words about holistic medicine. It proves that everybody is coming back to the feeling that we have to be more conscious of life as it moves in ourselves, of how we may change the flux of life with all the universe, and how we are to receive from nature itself or from heaven, because there is no difference between heaven and nature in the Chinese meanings. We have to be faithful to some inner indication which we call our own proper nature, and to know that it has been given by our ancestors. The cult of the ancestors is part of medicine, an appreciation of the environment is part of medicine, and a ritual for disposing of the body of a dead person is part of medicine. Everything is part of medicine if we take the Chinese view that medicine is just governing life in ourselves. But it may happen that it goes astray, perhaps for reasons inscribed in our personal genetics. The term genetics is not given as such in the Chinese classics, but they know that we come from a stock of something. Life may go astray because of the environment, or because our family is not stable. This affects us and there is some somatization. The Chinese know that all deviation of *qi* comes from the fact that we exhaust ourselves. We overdo things, we drink too much beer or wine, or something like that.

So everything is within the field of Chinese medicine if we understand that the governing of life is really proper to medicine, and that governing life in oneself or in a patient is just the individual aspect of that medicine. A physician who is treating a patient is only life treating life. So mutual understanding, and a willingness coming from both sides is of the essence. This is the answer, because it is important to engage oneself in the treatment.

I would also say nothing against the Occidental formation of medicine. We have here friends who pertain to both systems. So it is not that we oppose one way with the other, but we can say that in Occidental medicine it is easier to treat a person without engaging oneself in the treatment, and without the acceptance of the patient. There are lots of problems of medical ethics. What does it mean to engage oneself with another person? Are we engaging ourselves so much that two people merge into one? I think not. But I suppose that we should proceed in such a way in treating each patient that we can disengage ourselves too.

These are just a few indications of how we consider Chinese medicine in the European School of Acupuncture. This is nothing other that reading the texts as they present themselves. So if somebody asks 'Is there a good translation of the Nan jing or the Lei jing or the Nei jing or the Ling shu?' we should say 'Yes, they are excellent, but they are not useful'. They are excellent from the point of view of the man who has done the job, but the problem is not whether the translation is good. The problem is that nothing can be done with a Chinese text of the classical period, carefully preserved and transmitted to us, except to get back to the mind of the people of that time and to successive generations of writers and readers and practitioners. We have to forget the translation and come back to the text. We have to try and put our own mind and perception of life into understanding the text. Then the trouble is that if I want to express the feelings I have from my own translation, I come back to the same difficulty of language. I would say that the fact that a translation is good or bad depends not so much on the translator as on how you perceive the cultural difference between the Chinese when they were writing and your own modern English expression. As long as you are unable to bridge those two extremes a translation itself can remain good or bad, they are meaningless without explanation.

So what I propose to do in this seminar is proceed slowly. We want to just present a few items to give the feeling of how the Chinese text is really an expression of something we already know from our own personal, bodily consciousness. And this is not specific to Chinese medicine. There is a common understanding of things which is not always expressed. We are all living beings, and we give life one way or another, generating children, transmitting what we are and so on. We all know this. Reading Su wen chapter 8 we just want to see what our feeling of heart is, what our feeling of liver is, and so on. Is it possible that the Chinese, considering a living person, have a different appreciation of life than I myself have? I am sure that the Chinese of old and ourselves today are confronted with the same life. We have our way of expressing it, the Chinese had their's. Neither is better than the other. But in as much as our ways are highly sophisticated, complicated and overloaded with technical words, we may no longer see the functioning of the liver. In as much as the Chinese retain the most simple approach to the function of something arising in spring, seen in the wind and in the leaves and branches on trees, in as much as they preserve more than we do of the excellence and the specificity of very simple facts of life, they are closer to the medical truth than others. We have to humbly return to the text and try through that to see the real condition of life, both in ourselves and in treating patients.

THE FIRST CHAPTERS OF THE SU WEN

Claude Larre: Chapter 8 is a remarkable chapter. As far as I have understood, reading the Chinese text in a very poor manner compared to Elisabeth, chapter 8 is an eight-fold chapter. This seems not to be a great discovery in itself, but it has its importance. The first chapter gives the totality of life, and chapter 8 is also the totality of life. The first chapter is about longevity, not the extension of life as such, but the richness, the fullness and the extension of life in a saintly man, as provided by heaven or nature. Unfortunately something went wrong, and man was no longer able to reach one hundred years of age. A more important and a more obscure problem is why, even if we could reach one hundred years, a woman cannot give birth after seven periods of seven years, and a man can no longer father children after eight periods of eight years? This is very perplexing. I am not going to make an analysis of chapter 1, I just want you to recall that the first consideration of the Chinese in the Su wen is on this subject. There must be something very precious in life when it is pure. Then something went wrong, and we do not even know if it was a human crime or a heavenly decree which was responsible for the alteration of this power of life.

So, the first consideration is of life itself, and the potentiality of life. This is also a very clever introduction of Daoist concepts, since although what has been said is about ordinary men, there are also men and women of excellence, saintly persons. They are Daoists, and they are able to overcome the difficulty that life may be long, but it is not fertile beyond a certain time.

Life is taken whole, round as a ball, like the dark pearl of Huang di, the Yellow Emperor. He was always looking for this ball of life, this obscure pearl, which he lost somewhere. What this means is that humankind has lost the power to arrange life normally, and even the Yellow Emperor with all his knowledge is no longer able to find the secret of vitality in life. He knows more than anybody else, but he has to consult on this question of how life goes, or where life is, and that is the reason why the Nei jing is presented to us in the form of dialogues between the master, Qi Bo, (it is mainly Qi Bo although there are other people) and the man responsible for all life under heaven, the Yellow Emperor. Heaven is blue, but beneath heaven is yellow because it is the earth. And every creature, man, animal or plant, is the responsibility and kingdom of Huang di. He looks at this question, because although he knows the doctrine, he does not know the explanations well enough. But in a way this is not true. He pretends not to know enough in order that the exposition comes from another. This is typical of Chinese ways. The master knows, the disciples do not know, and sometimes even the master does not know, and then the disciple has to instruct him. But between Qi Bo and Huang di who is the master? Nobody knows since Qi Bo is a master and Huang di is the emperor. So is it true that the master will instruct the emperor or that the emperor will preserve the doctrine that the master will explain?

Chapter 2 is some sort of balancing of this wholeness of life through the mechanical device of Chinese thinking which is *yin yang* (陰 陽). I do not say concept or conception because that is so abstract and does not describe the phenomenon as it is reflected in the Chinese way of expression. The *yin yang* divides the ways the universe moves on itself, which they call *tian yun* (天 運).

Elisabeth Rochat: Heavenly distribution of influx.

Claude Larre: Yes, that is a very good translation. There is never just one translation for a Chinese expression! The only sure thing is that there is heaven, and there is a motion which is regular, like some sort of transportation of something. Under heaven's influence everything is transported somewhere. This general circulation, this natural motion of the universe may then be divided into two aspects, the *yin* aspect and the *yang* aspect. Aspects of what? Of *qi* (氣). There is some arising and some falling back of the *qi*. To rise in order to fall, and to fall in order to rise, that makes circulation. It is so high that we cannot perceive the essence of it. It is so universal that everything, everybody, every animal and every plant is affected and is under the same natural movement of *tian yun* (天 運).

The progression of this is seen through the four seasons. Thus the four seasons are not just four times in the year, they are four different aspects of the *tian yun* which we see very clearly as spring, summer, autumn and winter. Spring manifests itself everywhere as some beginning of life or renewing of the beginning of life, pertaining to the *tian yun*. This inner seed of transformation is visible, and through the different aspects of this visibility we can detect what we cannot express - some sort of spirit of spring.

The same is true for summer. The movement between spring and summer is progress. Summer takes what has been started and progresses along the line up to an acme, to the highest point of that progress, and then suddenly, in order to protect life and to protect the universe, it has to reverse its movement. So on some uncertain morning in the autumn time, the quality of air is very different. It is shocking. Something has started to reverse. It means that the *yin* which has been there but covered, unable to manifest itself except as a hidden, sustaining power, is now able to arise in its own right. Therefore the *yang* is receding. But there is no *yin* without *yang*, and there is not the slightest difference of constitution in *yin* and *yang*, only a difference in aspect. So the unity of the universe is such that *yin* and *yang* merge in that unity.

Then what we say of *yin* we should say in reverse terms of *yang*. It is a perfect parallel. But what we see in nature, in the fields, in the air, on the earth and so on, has special connotations.

The Book of Odes collects songs on the four seasons in the countryside which are very ancient, and historically speaking it is impossible to say when the Chinese first started this division with the unity which we call the *yin yang* effect. We know it is a genuine, and very solid doctrine. So if the connection between chapter 1 and chapter 2 is not evident to you it is just because we only call it evident when the logic of the text goes according to the ways we expound things ourselves. The normal pretension of an Occidental mind says that the Chinese are very illogical in their presentation, but on a deeper level we understand that chapter 1 and chapter 2 are about the same process, seen in the unity and seen divided into contrasted aspects. But the division does not alter the unity of life at all.

Then we move to chapter 3. Heaven is a life-giving power, so to say *yang qi* (陽氣) or *tian qi* (天氣) is usually the same thing. There is no *yang qi* unless it comes from heaven. But does *yin qi* (陰氣) come from heaven too? Yes, it does, since the nature of heaven may be divided into *yin* and *yang*. Heaven is responsible for autumn and winter just as much as for spring and summer. But the initiative for life, the life-giving power is of *yang* quality, and this *yang* quality has to be understood in the general flux of the universe within a man.

So in chapter 3 we start with some distinction of how *yang* is in nature, and what sort of power *yang* is when heaven is not retaining its own power. When *yang* is external, giving life, we can understand. We see the shining light of the sun, we feel the warmth, and we perceive in ourselves this sense of life. But sometimes heaven retains this *yang* power for an internal use. Then, like a man who is closing a door, there is no communication with the outside. Is that proof that there is nothing inside? On the contrary, it is not. So heaven has two ways of dealing with *yang*. It can give it out or not, and if heaven no longer gives the *yang* sustaining power then even the largest trees will decay and dry up. But sometimes there are saintly people who have kept enough life in themselves to give to all creatures until heaven opens the door and gives again. That is the role of saintly people. They provide enough stamina for a time, and life is possible. Then heaven pours down its power again and everything is bright. This is the Daoist concept of the role of certain people.

So in chapter 3 the question of the way the *yang* is moving is very deftly described, at dawn, at noontime, and in decline. But all this division of *yang* according to time is not made by time. Time is itself made by *yang*. We always have to think of things from an angle that we are not used to. What we know is what we know only in our own civilization, and maybe there is another way. Then we come to the question of how the *yang qi* in man may be expressed because it is contained somewhere. The end of the chapter is very nice, it says that this *yang qi* has to be sustained by some nutrition. It has to nourish itself through the five flavours or tastes, the *wu wei* (五味).

Then we proceed to chapter 4. Chapter 4 is a further organization of chapter 3. We know this life-giving force, but how is it organized in nature, on earth and in creating the human body? And how is the normality of this life seen through the divisions of the body? To be human with a body is just to be an expression on the fourth level of the *yang* virtue of heaven as contrasted with the supporting *yin qi*. We have seen that chapter 2 was talking more on the level of heaven and earth, producing the four seasons. Now here we are concentrating on the place between these two levels. Mankind is at the crossing of heaven and earth. So we just take what has been said in chapter 2, and duplicate that in making chapter 4. The organization is not so much organization of so-called time, but of so-called space. Space, that is, for the distribution of *yang,* and myself being a special, individual space for the distribution of the *yang* virtue of heaven. This is normality. But we know that normal things sometimes may go astray, and this gives scope for the acupuncturist in trying to restore them to normality!

You just have to find the path of life and restore the ways, in order that everything will be respected. You have to govern life to help the poor person back to normality. If there is too much of something you just discard it, and if there is lack of energy everywhere you have to call on the more profound energy which was stored from birth and which was completed by the *zong qi.* You have to restore the essences through the organization of life which is proper to that individual. Life knows its ways since the ways have been created by life. There is no difference between being a living person and being an organized body.

The organized body is the external face of the living strength of the living power, and it would be impossible to have the living power without a place for it. That is the very clever way the Chinese have built a body for a spirit, the spirit is given by heaven, and results in an individual appearance.

At this point we need to go towards organization and chapter 5. It is the chapter where, for the first time, the generality of life which has been exposed in the first four chapters is now presented with a spinning movement. Something is taking place here through the distribution by five. What is five? What is organization? Five and organization are the same thing. The process of organization is necessarily by five. It is no use calling on numerology. Numerology is a separate teaching. Here we are just extracting from what we see in the text. When we see that the Chinese are speaking of longevity in chapter 1, of a balance giving the flux of life in chapter 2, the *yang qi*, in chapter 3, the dispersion in chapter 4, and the organization in chapter 5, then we understand that numbers are a very high expression of what is done under heaven's rule. Then what about six and seven?

Elisabeth Rochat: Chapter 6 is the appearance of the *qi* differentiated in man. That is to say, the way in which the *qi* which will be *tai yang* (太 陽), *shao yang* (少 陽), *yang ming* (陽 明), *tai yin* (太 陰), *jue yin* (厥 陰) and *shao yin* (少 陰), is differentiated. It is the way in which these six forms are linked to the unity of the *qi* in a being, and are just the continually differentiated expression of the many parts of the form.

In chapter 7 we arrive at the emergence of manifestation in the form of pathology, because we are in a medical treatise, and seven is traditionally a number where we see something appear. In certain texts that are not concerned with medicine but with the life of man and with philosophy, in the seventh chapter we will see the apperance of the essences and spirits that form the vitality of man. But here in a medical text this will be in the form of pathological manifestations flowing from the presentation that has been made before. So in chapter 7 we see a dysfunctioning which is not very precise but rather general. For example, the way in which a disturbance in life at a very deep level will lead to death because one is no longer in tune with the great patterns which have been given before.

Chapters 1, 2, 3 and 4 form the first set of chapters. If we consider the title of each chapter we can make some further remarks. In the title of these first chapters we have the characters for heaven, authenticity and *qi*.

Claude Larre: We saw things very clearly up to chapter 5. Then when we come to chapter 6 it is just taking chapter 3 again, with the *yang*, life-giving *qi* from heaven. There we see this not in the universe in general but through six, three *yang* and three *yin qi*. So, just as chapter 4 was a duplication of chapter 2, so chapter 6 is the duplication of what we saw in chapter 3, with the insistence on the *yang qi* but with the presence of the *yin qi* behind it. It is quite normal that after presenting the *yang qi* in chapter 3, we should find it again with *shao yang*, *tai yang* and *yang ming*, along with the *yin qi*. If we look at the constitution of the numerology we see that three *yin* and three *yang* make six modulations of *qi* and that this number six is just the number of the chapter where this matter is treated. That is the normality. It is the silent work in the body. But if there is a manifestation, then it is *bing* (病), disease. If something manifests it is just because a disease is preparing itself to appear, and that has to be said in chapter 7, not in chapter 6.

So when we are in texts other than for medicine what is normal is that we would use chapter 7 for the expression of life. But it is always dangerous if life expresses itself when it is not in a healthy condition. When life is manifesting itself it is because life is declaring war somewhere. And when life is declaring war in yourself, we call that disease.

Now let us look at the characters of the chapter titles very quickly.

Chapter 1
Shang gu tian zhen lun

上　古　天　真　論

Shang gu (上 古) means 'during antiquity', or a concept related to antiquity. It is an expression of the authenticity, *zhen* (真), which is given by heaven, *tian* (天). We are talking of longevity because we are talking of the authenticity of the flux of life. If we are not observing the rules then we are no longer authentic, we are no longer under heaven's influence and we may thereby shorten our lives.

Chapter 2

Si qi tiao shen da lun

四 氣 調 神 大 論

The four seasons are only the four breaths (*si qi* 四 氣), which are the divisions of *yin yang* manifesting on the fourth level. And, using our spirits (*shen* 神), we should harmonize (*tiao* 調) ourselves with the external conditions which are mostly the atmospheric conditions. In spring there are rules, in summer there are rules, in autumn and winter there are rules to be observed. That is the main subject of the chapter.

Chapter 3

Sheng qi tong tian lun

生 氣 通 天 論

Heaven (*tian* 天) freely communicates (*tong* 通) through its authentic power, generating (*sheng* 生) people through its own spirit. The spirit that is in *qi* (氣), the breath of heaven given to you, makes you a heavenly person. There is no distinction between heaven and you when you have the authentic spirit given with the authentic breath.

Chapter 4

Jin kui zhen yan lun

金匱真言論

This doctrine has to be preserved in a very precious box. Looking at the title of the chapter it is now possible to see what Elisabeth has been talking about, organizing life inside the body, and the disease of people who are not observing the process of life in their organized body.

Chapter 5

Yin yang ying xiang da lun

陰陽應象大論

This is a great treatise, *da lun* (大論), on how all phenomena correspond to the very well-known *yin yang* highest manifestations of the aspects of life. *Yin yang* is always the same thing as life, but it is a distribution in contrast with life. It is the highest enveloping of life, and yet has the highest opposing qualities of life. So under this parenthesis there are always many opposing aspects, and this is used to understand how life is organized in detail. This chapter has 1,985 characters, it is one of the most extensive treatises in all the book. So we understand that it is talking of organization in all aspects, from heaven down to the smallest detail.

Chapter 5 is such a long chapter because it moves from the highest consideration to the minutest consideration, and finally gives a view to treatment, for example, how with some sort of acidity or sourness you may correct and balance the bodily disposition. Chapter 5 moves from the *yin yang*, down through all sorts of considerations to the actual practice of using one of the five elements to counterbalance some distortion in the specific, individual life. It goes through the five element system, down the chain of organization, to treatment. This is the reason why it is the longest chapter in the first two series.

Chapter 6

Yin yang li he lun

陰 陽 離 合 論

This is the treatise, *lun* (論), on how the *yin yang* govern the six *qi*. When we say three *yang qi* or three *yin qi*, we are just saying how *yin* and *yang* inside the six modulations which constitute the individual body are working one with the other, where they make their differentiation and where they make their reunion. This is to separate, not in a bad way, but in a good way. This is the specificity of six, and this is the synthesis, the playing together of six.

Chapter 7

Yin yang bie lun

陰 陽 別 論

Seven is the separation. In the six relations, *liu he* (六 合), which is a very important expression in Chinese, when something goes wrong, when something is parting and taking its own way, then disease may arise.

I understand that it is taking a lot of time to make this preliminary explanation in order that we may enter Su wen chapter 8, but at least you may perceive that chapter 8 comes in its proper place. It relies on chapters 7, 6, 5, 4, 3, 2 and 1. And now you must understand that chapter 7 relies on chapters 6, 5, 4, 3, 2 and 1! Then you realise that two, four and six are constructed by duplication of two by four, and by addition of this and that. But playing on numbers does not give any information. Whenever you get information you are able to play with the numbers and it helps to understand the organization in your mind. This logic of life was very strong in the second century BC, everything is organized with *yin yang* and the five elements. This logic is not dead logic. Just as a botanist would open a flower and would open the leaves and would count how many of this and how many of that, he would understand that numerology is essential to the organization of life. But it is better to always fall back onto numerology and not to proceed from numerology to the actual facts.

Elisabeth was saying that we have to take the first four chapters as a whole, a section. The Chinese word is *juan* (卷). *Juan* means a volume, and within the volume there are discussions which are the *lun* (論). *Lun* means to expose and to discuss a question. The four first chapters are the first *juan*, which is more or less the highest level of discussion of the flux under heaven's guidance. The second section is made up of only three chapters, 5, 6 and 7. It also consists of *lun*, discussions. There are big discussions, *da lun* (大 論), and these are under *yin yang*. *Yin yang* are the two first characters in each chapter title. Then chapter 8 is the first chapter in the series which deals with the organs, the *zang* (臟).

So to sum all that up, we could say that the first section is about the heavenly power expanding itself. Then, what is the secret movement within that heavenly power? It is the *yin yang* effect, which is not seen itself, but which is seen through other phenomena. When you see light and obscurity, it is a further development of *yin yang*. It is not *yin yang*. *Yin yang* itself cannot be observed. But everything that you can observe must fall into *yin yang*. After this consideration of *yin yang* life is able to be constructed within an individual.

Then it is time to see how life is operating. Life operates with the inner part of oneself, which is comprised of the five *zang*. When we speak of spiritual life in Europe, we are talking of something which is, in our minds, separated from the needs of the body. This is ridiculous! We are not angels. The most spiritual people usually eat, drink and sleep! When the Chinese talk of a spiritual person, they want to see what his ways of doing things are. They want him to be really human, and they know that the control of life has to be made through 'functions'. Function is a very awkward word. Function is very Western. We say things go this way or that way without seeing any visible thing that we call a function. But for the Chinese, when they say *zang* they are not talking of functions. They are talking of the secret ways, very close to nature, which control all the effects of life. So one point of misunderstanding which is common when you are talking with a physician of Occidental medicine and you are talking of the liver, the stomach, the lungs or the heart, is that he will see only the organ. But when you are talking of the liver in Chinese medicine you are talking of spring, or wood, and eventually of liver.

The five organs come in the series of chapters from 8 to 12. There are four chapters on the five *zang* to give further information on the central part of activity in human life.

Now, starting with the translation and commentary of this chapter we are speaking of the twelve charges. I do not say 'officials', although 'officials' is the usual translation in English. The Chinese text is *shi er guan* (十 二 官), and there is no translation that is an equivalent. If I say 'officials' you see a person. If I say 'charges' you see a way of operating with a responsibility towards the highest authority, maybe a king or heaven, so I prefer that. Someone else might say charges is not good at all, and officials is the word. The contest is without end. The point is to accept the word and see what you can do with it.

Elisabeth was just saying that the term *guan* (官) comes later on. At the beginning of the text it is just *shi er zang* (十 二 藏). *Zang* means to treasure or to store preciously. These *guan* are taken by the *zang* (臟), and they are qualified to discharge the duty of their charges. That is the general subject of chapter 8.

SU WEN CHAPTER 8

Ling lan mi dian lun
靈 蘭 秘 典 論

Ling lan (靈 蘭) is one expression. *Mi dian* (秘 典) is another. According to the usual translation, it means The Secret Treatise of the Spiritual Orchid. This is a canonical text not available to everyone, but reserved for specific people. The Spiritual Orchid (*ling lan* 靈 蘭) was the name of the library of the Yellow Emperor, the Temple of the Spiritual Orchid. It means that inside the palace there was a special place, the personal library of the emperor, which was called the Spiritual Orchid. The reason for this very special name is that an orchid is a plant full of life. Our word orchid refers to the Greek language where it is *orche*, something to do with the power of life itself.

In old Chinese mythology different legends tell how the orchid is able to give life. Therefore with the orchid we have a feeling of spiritual life, but this is much more clearly expressed by the addition of *ling* before the orchid, *lan*. *Ling* (靈) is spiritual, with the connotation of the freshness of activity in life. It comes from on high and it just needs somebody with open hands to accept this gift from heaven. The earth accepts heaven's gift which is pouring down, especially with spring rainfall.

The upper part of the character *ling* (靈) is radical number 173 (*yu* 雨), meaning four drops coming from the canopy of heaven. You can see the canopy and you can see the four drops. It is used not only for rain but for anything coming down from heaven such as snow, ice, and all sorts of mist. Underneath are shamanesses (*wu* 巫) with three mouths, meaning that they are crying to heaven. They are imploring heaven to give rain. The character is built with three parts, and the power of the spirits is expressed by the fact that they manifest themselves only under certain conditions. The imploring from the sorceresses is needed, and it is efficient enough to call down rain from heaven. That is magic!

Just from the title itself you can see that the teaching is solemn and on the highest level. It is basic for the knowledge of life in a human being. So it is secret, it is simple, and it is reserved for people who are initiated. The difficulty is in our minds, in the fact that we have not received any light from heaven. Somebody with illumination will find very easy that which somebody without illumination will find very difficult.

There must be a reason why the function or the charges of the twelve *zang* are treated in the chapter with the number eight. We must find a connection between eight and twelve. The winds are organized with the eight system. Space and time are the medium where life is flowing in all directions. It is through the wind that life moves freely everywhere. Then, if we are instructing people on how the twelve *zang* are operating, the best thing is to take this construction of twelve to the origin, which is the eight winds. This is the principle of organization. There is no materialization of life as such when we are at the level of eight. We have to wait for the coming of the number twelve to perceive that this higher organization is now taking place on the level of the very specific individual. Before the human being, before there are meridians, before there is the organisation of the year, there is something higher, with less determination, and that is the eight winds. So the eight winds project themselves and make a year with twelve months. And when they make the circulation or propulsion of life, then it is according to the twelve meridians. Or, built more basically, it would be the twelve *zang*. Twelve *zang*, twelve meridians or twelve months, are all just a projection of the eight.

There is no figuration, no materialization of the eight winds themselves. Even when we say winds, we must know that they are winds without any breath or motion, because the Chinese concept of wind is wind without motion, but which may then be put into motion. Motionless air is full of the eight winds. And, of course, the quality of wind is not seen except when the wind is in motion. So there are specific winds, and there are eight of them, and when the eight winds are in motion all together there is no motion because they are all contradicting themselves. When somebody is under the influence of a specific wind in motion this will only be seen in the individual person at the twelve levels.

This chapter is very short, only six hundred and something characters, and it is divided into three parts: a question from Huang di, rather a lengthy answer from Qi Bo and a very short conclusion. The fundamental question is unique, what is the meaning of *zang* (臟)? The question is more specific in saying what is a *zang* when you speak of twelve *zang*, and how are they expressed in a hierarchy?

Question: I am confused between *zang* (臟) and *cang* (藏).

Elisabeth Rochat: It is basically the same character, the meaning of which is storage. When you use it as a verb you have *cang* (藏) and when you want to designate the organs you have the radical for flesh, or part of the body, and it is *zang* (臟). But in the ancient texts sometimes the radical for flesh is not put in, yet it still has the same meaning of organ.

Claude Larre: Around 210 BC the prime minister of Qinshi Huangdi reorganized the writing in the empire. Calling it *li shu*, official writing, he devised a system of writing, and at the same time he unified the characters which were used by all the different kingdoms existing before the empire. From that time on people were more and more inclined to put additional radicals in the characters to distinguish them more easily. So we can say that during the Han dynasty, the writing of Chinese characters had acquired a normalization and that some people would add more radicals than others, for example the radical for flesh, 肉 (or in composition 月), in the character *zang*.

Elisabeth Rochat: The so-called five *zang* are only a way to actively store or to keep.

Claude Larre: The profound meaning of the *zang* is that their charge, *guan* (官), is to store the essences. They take from food the nourishing part, and they refine it up to the point where it is at the same level of constitution as the specific nature of a particular individual. And then they store it. In other words it is impossible to store things which are not on the same level as your own personal constitution. The essences are stored because they are refined. Between essences, storage and *zang* there is no difference. Essences are the particulars on which life relies. But to be able to get essences you need a systematic organization of your deeper self. And your deeper self is your five *zang*. If there are five, it means that there are five ways to acquire and separate essences. So storing preciously means both separation and refinement and so on. The complexity of the Chinese characters stems from their richness, but in your mind you have to record the many, many different uses which combine to make life possible.

To analyse the character *zang* further, the inner part is *chen* (臣), the obedient servant, or with a pejorative meaning, a slave. This is a person who has been taken prisoner in war. The Chinese separate, refine and eliminate, and they take from amongst those prisoners the most able! These are taken to the court where they are used as ministers. This is more or less what the Romans did with the Greeks, at a different level, when they installed the pedagogical system. The noble Romans used to have a Greek slave at home to teach arts and literature to their children. In the same way all peoples take individuals who have brains and store them, like the Americans who buy in Europe. The character *chen* (臣) shows a man bent forward, towards the lord, waiting for orders. This is incorporated into the character so it means that the *zang* are servants of life (cf. Wieger Lessons 82 E and 78 B).

Question: What is the relationship between the twelve *zang* and the eight winds?

Claude Larre: The answer will be seen clearly later on. Right now we can just say that the twelve *zang* are twelve because they are regulated by five which is the number for organization. We have to come from twelve to five to understand the relation between the five *zang* and the twelve *zang*. When you understand that the twelve are just a development of the five, then the question is what is the relation between the five *zang* and the eight winds? So before answering your question about what the relation is between the eight winds and the twelve *zang*, we have to ask the question about why you speak of twelve *zang* when usually we speak of five *zang*? There are twelve *zang* because there are five *zang* and six *fu*, and there is something between eleven and twelve. When we talk of the five *zang* we are just talking of the five *zang* in contrast with the six *fu*. When we take the five *zang* and the six *fu*, since we know that although they are eleven they have twelve charges, so the best way to speak of that is to say twelve *zang*. The functions are twelve even if the so-called officials are only eleven. But the question of why eleven or why twelve is a question which is difficult in itself. The duplication of functions for the heart is not simple if you do not really know what the place of the heart in the organism is. So it is not convenient right now to make a distinction between eleven and twelve.

To come back to the question of the eight winds, they are a very high concept compared with the twelve. Twelve is some sort of projection. The eight winds project themselves for organizing life in man, or organizing life in the universe. The winds are at the level of gods. They are life-giving. And if there are eight it is just because there are four directions, and the energy of the four directions on the move has to be seen by duplication. We had earlier some examples of how, when something is on one level, there is also another corresponding level. So if the first is two then the other will be four, or if the first is three then the other will be six. So if the organization of the *qi*, the breaths on earth, is by four, then a further organization of the power of life between heaven and earth will be the eight winds. And the further organization of four through eight will be twelve.

This may seem surprising at first, but with time you will find it very normal that duplication or triplication makes a change of level. The highest is the simplest. One, two, three, four and five are very simple. But six is related to three, and eight is related to four, and twelve is necessarily related to three and four. So twelve is an excellent number because it is the synthesis of presentation by three and four.

Elisabeth Rochat: This character *zang* (臟) is about preserving and conserving what is precious to life, and what is essential to life are the *qi* and the essences. In the Nei jing it is related to this meaning of refining and preserving the *qi* that we find this character associated with various different numbers. But what does it mean to associate the character with them? It never means that there are more than five ways for a person to refine the *qi* and the spirits. Five means that there is a life that centres itself on one point in order to be manifest, because five is the way in which life is expressed or comes into being on earth, beneath heaven. It is the meeting point and the gathering. In the character the cross shows four points (五), ie. the number four, which gather towards the middle into a fifth one, and that is the number five. A more archaic way of writing the number five places the permutation of the *qi* between heaven above and earth below, and the crossing of the two, the midpoint, is represented by number five. In four we have the four directions and the four seasons, creating the dimensions of space and time. Number five is the dimension in which these permutations have an action.

This is why mankind is seen as a crossing of these energies of east, west, north and south, of the seasons, and all the space and time between heaven and earth, and this is why number five represents the knot of life. This is why we have five elements, five flavours and five *zang*. And this is why the spirits that are in me and which make my life, spread themselves in five ways in order to manifest my being, expressing themselves through the five *zang*. So the *zang* are to me what the directions are for the cosmos - the reference. These *zang* are the receptacles for my spirit and the way to govern my life in the deepest part of my being. This is why, with this meaning there are five and only five *zang*. Once this is established all sorts of other permutations that can take place.

Claude Larre: I would like to look at things from another point of view. Take, for example, the United Kingdom. How many powers are there? There is the sovereignty, the queen, the highest tradition and all that. There is the prime minister, very different from the queen, but with a lot of power. Then take the two Houses of Parliament, in a way being nothing to do with the prime minister. They are for deliberating, and they are the legislative power not the executive power. They are just for making laws. Then take the people who preside at the supreme court. They represent the queen, but the queen cannot really interfere. The judges are independent, they are a judicial power. So I am referring to four powers, but we could add public opinion as a fifth, because it is impossible to govern against public opinion. Thus in the life of the United Kingdom there are five *zang*, all essential to make things move. You cannot add and you cannot subtract from that core of power, but you may say that some special responsibility is located here or there. Then you may add more powers, but you must integrate them under these five because it is only the five which move the nation ahead.

Elisabeth Rochat: If you were talking about four *zang* you would be talking about the stomach, large intestines, bladder and small intestines because these are related to digestion and the external contribution to nourishment. You could also be talking about the head, the eyes and ears, the mouth and the region in the middle of the chest, which are all places where the *qi* has to accumulate in a precious way in order to be able to think, see, hear and eat. These are key points of life. For six you would be referring to the five *zang* to which we would add the double function of the kidneys. The kidneys are counted as two. They have their own refining and accumulation in the context of the five *zang* related to water, the will and so on, but on the other side they have *ming men* (命 門), the authentic breaths (*zhen qi* 真 氣), and the original water and fire, and this is what is counted for six. The number six accounts for the origin of life and its maintenance and its future. Twelve is the number by which life is ordered and organized, for example in twleve months of the year. The twelve *zang* refers to the five *zang* and the six *fu*.

Claude Larre: The true meaning of the term *fu* (府) is auxiliary. The auxiliary has the same regime as the principal, so if you call the principal *zang* you may call the auxiliary *zang*. If you have the lord mayor and the deputy mayor, both are mayors of the city. But when you want to really express the power of the mayor you say lord mayor, but when you are on practical business you usually go to the deputy mayor. Food always goes to the deputy mayor, and then once it is prepared, the lord mayor acts on it!

Elisabeth Rochat: The twelve *zang* represent the whole work done by the essences and *qi* in relation to regeneration of vitality through food and breathing, as well as to the deep refining and preserving of the *qi*. There is a need for there to be essences and *qi* in order for the spirit to manifest in the human body. So twelve represents the total ordering and regulation of the whole being. We are at the eighth chapter because eight represents the overall dispersion of these essences and *qi*, whether by the eight winds or the eight extraordinary meridians.

Claude Larre: You must be very aware that when a number is used, like eight, to say this is either through the eight winds or the eight extraordinary meridians, it is not really either/or. It just looks like that. We are forced by our own language to say it is this or that, or it is this through that. Whenever there is a number, everything coming through the number is present in life. The number in itself is powerful enough to harmonize and unify all the *qi*. So whenever I hear eight, I understand that it is at once the eight winds and the eight extraordinary meridians. Referring to a text, I have to know the context to see if it is alluding to the winds or the extraordinary meridians. If the text is not actually referring specifically to them, it is not that they are not present. The reason it is so confusing in reading books, or difficult to listen to some teaching is that everybody is freely using language more or less as they choose. But we have to know that the Chinese tradition is fixed, and what we have been saying in terms of the tradition does not admit of a lot of explanation. It is like weaving, if you change the motion, it is no longer weaving.

Elisabeth Rochat: You cannot talk of eight functions in response to essences and *qi* in this chapter. Eight means that there are essences and *qi* spread out everywhere, and the number twelve represents just how this presence of essences and *qi* is going to be manifest. This is why the emperor asks for an explanation about these twelve *zang*, and he asks his question in relation to how these essences and *qi* relate to each other. What is the hierarchy that stands out amongst the *zang*? Because when there is a state where the *zang* inter-relate with each other, there cannot be order unless there is hierarchy.

Claude Larre: How is it possible that eight is twelve, that eight in the mist equals twelve in the distinct? Eight in the mist is just on high, where everything is the breath of winds or the harmony of heaven. But if you want to see that in a distinct manner, inside the life of an individual, you have to take the twelve to represent the eight, even though they are not in the same state. Eight is a higher level, a level where things are in the chaotic state of heaven, where essences are here and there. But when essences are organized in man, they are no longer here and there. When Elisabeth was alluding to the extraordinary meridians she was alluding to the fact that at the beginning of life there are not twelve meridians, there are meridians but there are only eight because at that time the being in the making is still organized by the highest state of essences. Then progressively the twelve take the place of the eight, although the eight remain the primary organization and the twelve are on the surface. As children or as adults we keep the organization of the eight extraordinary meridians to support our life. So the equation is absolutely true! Eight in the mist equals twelve in the distinct.

Elisabeth Rochat: This is why Qi Bo begins by saying to the emperor, 'What a huge question'. He answers by saying that he is going to take it step by step and slowly, and to put in a bit of order and proceed regularly and carefully.

THE HEART

xin zhe jun zhu zhi guan ye
shen ming chu yan

心者君主之官
神明出焉

The heart holds the office of lord and sovereign
The radiance of the spirits stems from it

Elisabeth Rochat: According to traditional Chinese etymologists the ideogram of the heart is the outline of the actual physical shape of a heart (cf. Wieger Lesson 107 A, phonetic 61). What is interesting about this character is that we have both the bowl or receptacle of the heart and the beginning of the features of communication with other parts of the body, and in particular with the other *zang*, via the aorta and the arteries. The heart is literally the emperor and sovereign of the body. The heart is at the centre of the kingdom, of the palace and of the Forbidden City, and is the one who has authority, and from whom all commands are issued. So the small lines in the heart character represent the movement outward towards the rest of the kingdom and the longer central stroke is the container.

Two characters represent the function or charge, and they present the two aspects of the heart. The first is *jun* (君), the heart as lord and sovereign, the heart being the centre. This is the heart as the one who has authority by nature and birthright, and whose very presence is a guarantee of order. The mere fact of its presence represents order and heaven. The second character, *zhu* (主), is the sovereign in action, or in the process of being acted out. So *jun* represents the natural, inborn authority, and *zhu* represents this authority in action. Thus the expression *xin zhu* (心 主), sometimes translated in English as heart governor, means the heart at work, acting as master, regulating the circulation and animation of life.

Claude Larre: We may say heart master or heart governor but not heart's governor, because the heart is the governor and is not being governed by anybody.

Elisabeth Rochat: In order for this authority to be exerted through the blood and through the life-giving network, the *mai* (脈), there must be a system of communication issuing from the heart. The system of relations and connections by which the heart communicates its orders to the *zang*, through the blood is called *xin bao luo* (心包絡). This is something imperceptible and very fine, it is not the arteries but some very subtle connection. The communication may travel through the blood and through the *mai*, through the enveloping tissues and membranes, but it is not at the same level of materialisation as them. If you look at the characters which make up this expression, in *luo* (絡) there is the silk thread which is attached to a link. This represents the fine and subtle system of relations and connection, the mesh of communications which relates to the heart. On the other hand you have in *bao* (包) the enveloping membranes surrounding the heart. This expression *xin bao luo* (心包絡) is often translated as heart protector or heart constrictor. It is the way in which the heart is protected by membranes and is in communication with the other *zang* by means of the network.

Claude Larre: I would just add one word. You may marvel at the fact that such profound and important things have been more or less mistranslated for such a long time! But you have to understand that the normal Chinese translation leads to two interpretations. Take the example of *xin zhu* (心 主), the heart governor. If you do not know what it is about you just look at the Chinese characters and two ways of translation are open. The most normal one is by determination: what sort of governor? The governor of the heart. But that is not sinology, it is just ordinary Chinese language translation. In classical Chinese the more usual determination would be to ask what aspect of the heart? And the answer is when the heart is governing.

It must be said that Soulié de Morant, Chamfrault and others did not always pay very much attention to these aspects of the classical text. Since it was new material they were quick to propose a translation, and although they probably knew what was behind it as far as theory was concerned they did not pay much attention to the way a sinological translation should be made. Now we are in a very difficult position after eighty to one hundred years of teaching on this, because it is difficult to propose a new translation. So we will just say heart master or heart as envelope and connections. But in teaching we must explain the difficulty, and warn people of the difference between the heart's master and the heart as master.

Elisabeth Rochat: It is always the heart itself which is the *zang*, you can not have a *zang* heart protector or heart master. It is only the heart which refines the spirit, and then manifests its double condition or dual role, its natural sovereignty on one hand and the exertion of its authority on the other.

With these two characters *jun* (君) and *zhu* (主) the Su wen represents the dual charge or office of the heart. The character for charge is *guan* (官), and it shows a place from which a particular authority is being exerted. The upper part of the character represents a roof and the lower part is a sort of construction. It relates to the place in a town where the officer in charge resides. The character later went on to represent the dignitary himself (cf. Wieger Lesson 86 C).

Claude Larre: There is something very exciting and interesting in looking at this character showing one building and another building in a yard. The two buildings are connected, and you can go from one to the other. They are different, but they are connected. Another character which is very similar to *guan* is *gong* (宮). This is a palace or important building, and is frequently seen in texts. *Zi gong* (子宮) is the uterus, the residence for children, and *nao gong* (腦宮) is the brain. The only difference in the characters is the one stroke linking the two buildings. In both characters it is a place where something operates. So a small difference in the characters makes a big difference in the meaning. But both of them show that it is always necessary to have a place from which to exert authority.

Question: Is the phenomenon of *xin xi* (心系) unique to the heart, or would each *zang* (臟) have a *xi* (系)?

Elisabeth Rochat: *Xin xi* (心系), the connections proper to the heart, is quite different. It is the particular network of relationships extending from the heart. The expression is in opposition to another one, *xin zhong* (心 中), the heart as the centre. The centre of the heart, or the heart as a centre, is a deep place for the life of man as a residence or palace for the spirit. And if the heart, as a centre, is injured, there there will inevitably be death.

The *xin zhong* (心 中) is where the meridian of the heart begins. After emerging from the central region of the heart it comes out and goes up to join with the system of connections of the heart, the *xin xi* (心 系). The meridian takes a dependent relation with the heart, not as centre because you cannot reach the vital centre and touch the residence of the spirit, but with the heart as connected to the other *zang*. This is because the only way you can touch the heart is in relation to its system of command and in its relationships with other *zang*. This may be via the *shao yin* (少 陰) of the hand, the meridian of the heart, or on the second meridian of the heart, the *xin zhu* (心 主), which is the heart exerting its authority on the circle of the five *zang*. But it is always the periphery of the heart, you can only reach the heart via its system of connections, or in its commanding position. You can never actually touch the *shen* (神), the spirits.

Claude Larre: Let me give two examples of this. Do you remember the fellow who got into the queen's bedroom? It was quite incredible, because it should not be possible for a private citizen to come into contact with the queen except through established systematic relationships, the *xi* (系). Another example is from France. The former president Giscard d'Estaing wanted to have breakfast with some street cleaners. He could call them and have breakfast with them, but they could not call him back and invite him to their own homes without going through the process of addressing a president. So we understand that when the sovereign is there, a connection between him and other parts of life is necessary.

Elisabeth Rochat: So sometimes it is said that the heart meridian itself does not have a *shu* (俞) point within the five elements because there can only be a series of five with the five *zang*, and what is related to the heart as a centre and the heart as lord will come out of this circle of the five elements. Therefore, there are two aspects of the heart, the one that is related to the other *zang*, and the one that is completely outside all of that. But it is the one that is outside of everything else that is actually the one which makes everything work, because if there were no spirits then nothing would work. There is a construction or building made in order to show that there is an authority which is exerted, and there are functionaries or ministers who are there in order to exert this authority. So if this authority is well effected and in good spirits, then life in the surrounding country will be well disposed. You see this in all Chinese stories.

If the heart exerts its authority as lord and sovereign in a good manner then this effect will spread throughout the empire. Hence the *shen ming* (神 明), the brilliance of the *shen*, can shine out. This means that the spirits that are kept and guarded in the heart, and which at the same time keep and guard the heart, can spread the light of virtue throughout the empire or the body. There is a brilliance and a radiance, which manifests everywhere. There is a liveliness in the person, which can be seen in the shine of the eye. It is a well-assured, lively, bright look. You see the pink, firm flesh and the penetration of the intelligence, and they are people who seem to radiate something that is difficult to qualify, like health or virtue. They seem to have presence. For example a saint radiates all the force or strength of the spirit and he has the same effect all around him, on vegetation, animals and people. Everyone will live better because of the effect of such a man, and when there are natural catastrophes, it is people like this who make sure that life survives on earth.

This is written in Su wen chapter 2, which is a medical text not a philosophical book. When you look at the body of an individual it is exactly the same story. If the spirits that are in the heart can communicate with the other *zang* then there is the same exceptional quality of life which can only be given by the spirits throughout the being. The spirits can manifest because they receive essences, *jing* (精). The spirits are like riders looking for good horses, and the essences are those horses, with the most choice essences going to the heart. The pre-heavenly, authentic or original essences, and all the essences that are then drawn from food, must be of good quality, because if not the blood is not as rich and all the bodily liquids will suffer. The *qi* will also suffer because it will not be able to draw as much from the essences, and at the same time the spirits are unable to manifest their direction and control. It would be like an empire where the roads are not well maintained, or there are strikes, and all that rapidly leads to decay.

Claude Larre: There is also an historical question of the tribute which was brought to the emperor. This was not only done to recognize that the emperor was higher than anyone else, but because it was a way to nourish the centre of power. All the country gave something to the court in order that the emperor and the people around him would be nourished, and it was the most refined products that were given. Barbarians from the occident, from the north and the south, came to the centre, and they brought elephant ivory tusks, or mechanical devices and so on, in order that the centre, where life on earth is preserved, would be nourished.

So the tribute has two functions. The first was to recognize that the Chinese court was higher than others, and the second was to show appreciation for life and to enable life to go on as it should because in order to let the people know that their tribute had been accepted, the Chinese court would then give twice as much from its own reserve to the donors. Thus the balance would be kept. They did this annually when they had conquered a country to impose their rule. Sometimes when they were not able to enforce it, they only accepted tribute every three years. In this case the givers did not want to give the impression to their own people that they were in submission to the Chinese court. If you consider all this on a political level then you can see the same thing at the level of the heart and the body, it being essential that every part of the body sends tribute to the centre. Then you understand that the connections of the heart, *xin xi* (心 系), are there not only to maintain order, but also to accept nourishment coming from all parts of the body, and to receive all that is necessary for the life of the heart.

The heart is not just a pump to move blood, it is the highest entity in human life. And it is very interesting to understand that morality, virtue and so on are understood by the Chinese not just as being in the field of religion for example, but as essential to keep the quality of life. This is the reason why we have to go and see wonderful scenery, be well rested, have good food and drink and all that, in order that life will be more and more refined. From this digesting of essences you are then in a position to distribute them.

Elisabeth Rochat: *Shen ming* (神 明), the radiance of the spirits, not only applies to medicine, it is an idea that belongs to all Chinese culture. It is found in the great texts of Daoism and Confucianism. We also have to add that if there is something that is shining and radiating, then this emission does not stem from an accumulation but from a void. It comes not from a piling up but from a potential space which is very refined. A void is not an absence or an emptiness. The void of the heart is a fundamental concept in China, and from that comes the idea that nothing must block communication and circulation from the heart to the whole being. Nothing must block the radiance of the spirits, and nothing must obstruct the orifices of the heart. The heart must be calm, tranquil and peaceful, and that then allows all the transformations which make up the life of the body.

Question: Why is *shen* (神) translated as 'spirits' and not 'spirit'?

Elisabeth Rochat: Because if you have it in the singular it gives you the impression that it is 'the' spirit. In the plural it gives more of the sense of a power of spiritual order. Put in the plural it implies something different from what we normally think of as spirit in the West. All the great European sinologists put it in the plural not the singular.

Question: So it is not the spirit in the sense that we Westerners see it?

Elisabeth Rochat: Yes it is, but not exactly.

Claude Larre: We can see that the character *shen* (神) is made with two parts. The left shows an oracle (示) (cf. Wieger Lesson 3 D). It means that the spirit has something to do with a cult: the cult of heaven, of mountains, marshes, rivers and so on.

Any specific form which is seen around us, every phenomenon is nothing other than the expression of the virtue of heaven and earth, and this virtue is greater than myself. So it might be safer for me to ask benevolence from this power, to welcome every sort of phenomenon which would come and benefit my life and protect me against other spirits. For that reason a cult is made for the emperor to give homage to heaven and earth, and for earth to give to the five mountains of China and to the rivers and so on. The other aspect of the spirits, seen on the right side of the character (申), is that they are like a scarf or a piece of material being stretched out in indefinite forms (cf. Wieger Lesson 50 C). So the root is found in the cult, and the external manifestation is like the slow gliding of the clouds, and all sorts of atmospheric condensations like mist and fog. The perception of the atmospherics of the inner forces of the universe which regulate everything everywhere, including our own heart, liver and lungs and so on, ensures that they are not separate from the spirits of the heart, liver and lungs. So it is normal, safe and good to be under the influence of the spirits and to have rituals, to know how to behave if something happens in oneself or if one comes across a manifestation of spirits. Everything is so mingled and inconsistent that a general name has to be found for these things when they come at a certain level, and when they are concerned with my heart and *zang* they are called *shen*.

Opposed to the *shen* there is a world of creatures of a lesser quality which are in charge of alimentation and waste, disposing of the body and so on, the *gui* (鬼). The character shows a large head, with something on the top. The *gui* have to be taken care of too. The *shen* (神) move in the air, but the *gui* (鬼) walk on the ground, so combining the *shen* and the *gui* you have all the spirits of the higher and lower levels. For convenience when we say spirits we are always referring to the *shen*, and when we have to deal with the *gui* we just say *gui* because it is not safe to call them bad names! You never know exactly how they would take it if you called them devils! If you say genii, genii is vague, but if you say *gui* it is very precise. You can also say *shen gui* (神 鬼) and *gui shen* (鬼 神) If you say *shen gui* it refers to the normal distribution, the higher and lower levels, but if you say *gui shen* it is less favourable because priority is given to the *gui*. So you see it is no longer possible to discuss whether it is spirit or spirits. A lot of problems are only the interference between our ways of thinking and the Chinese tradition. And the closer we come to the Chinese words, the less problems we have.

THE LUNG

肺

fei zhe xiang fu zhi guan
zhi jie chu yan

肺者相傅之官
治節出焉

The lung holds the office of minister and chancellor
The regulation of all rhythms stem from it

Elisabeth Rochat: Directly after the heart come the lungs. In Chinese it is really the lung, because it is one organ even though there are two lobes. The character *fei* (肺) is composed with the radical of the flesh on the left side (月), like most of the *zang* and *fu*. Only the heart and the triple heater do not have this flesh radical, and obviously this is not just by chance, but we will come back to that later. The other part of the character on the right represents plants which creep on the ground and which are continutally dividing into many, many branches. In this branching you have the idea of proliferation, abundance, and a certain violence and speed, the rapidity of the vital force which comes out like this. Some people have also made the connection between this diversification and branching out of the plant with the structure and fibres of the lungs.

Claude Larre: That is the reason why you see so many illustrations of the lungs in Chinese texts with the appearance of leaves. It is not etymology for the sake of etymology, it is the normal representation as seen in the mind.

Elisabeth Rochat: The lung holds a privileged place because it is found in the upper part of the body above the diaphragm, along with the heart. This does not seem to tell us very much at first, but the body that we have is the result of very ordered work which comes from the regulation of *qi* from heaven and earth. The situation or location of different parts of the body, on the left or on the right, above or below, will give an indication of the actual functions of the *zang* that are found in these specific places. Because heaven is above and earth is below, the fact that the head is high up in the body is an indication that it has the same quality as that which is most refined, meaning heaven.

We can do the same analysis for the other organs of the body by looking at their location in the trunk, and trying to see the hierarchy amonst the *zang*. If you could not make such deductions, then the body would not actually be an expression of the joining of heaven and earth. So it is for this reason that the lung, which is just next to the heart, is the minister and chancellor, and has the function of being the helper of the heart. The character *xiang* (相), which is translated as minister, also has a common meaning of reciprocity, or to reinforce an aspect of relations between two people.

Claude Larre: But this does not take out the hierarchy between the sovereign and minister. Just because they are on speaking terms does not mean that the minister may pretend to be some sort of sovereign, or that the king would be so silly as to look on the minister as only a friend. Disorder in all kingdoms, or in all life, just stems from this weakness in the prince or this arrogance in the minister, all of which can be seen throughout the history of China and other countries. So it is interesting to see that they chose *xiang* (相) and *fu* (傅), and if on giving explanations they pay attention to the fact that in other relationships reciprocity is made without taking notice of hierarchy, in this situation that would not do. As for the chancellor being a more external function than the *xiang*, we have the same relationship as with *jun* (君) and *zhu* (主) in reference to the heart. We have already seen that the inner self of the heart is the lord, but that the expression of that inner self is as master. In this sort of relationship there is always one sort of position, and then the expression coming out of that position. With the lung we have the minister, but the minister in acting with orders, ordinances, and so on, is in that aspect chancellor. The chancellor has to do with writing and stamping, while the minister confers with the prince, offers advice and opinions. But the hierarchy is preserved, and in the offices where the writing and administration is done, they wait for instructions, and it is the lung who, after consultation with the king, instructs the attendants on what to write. At that time he is acting as chancellor. It is very interesting to see that the lung is so powerful. Now we can understand why the beating of the heart and the rhythm of respiration are so interconnected, and that this is just the more external aspect of some sort of inner relation between the heart and lung which is exemplified in the relationship beteween the lord who is sovereign and the prime minister who is chancellor.

Elisabeth Rochat: In the couple made by sovereign and minister, heart and lung, the heart is considered a masculine or male *zang* and the lung is a feminine or female *zang*. This gives the same idea of the minister who is *yin* in relation to the sovereign who is *yang*. There is also another couple related to the vitality presided over by the heart and lung, and that is blood and *qi*. The lung governs or masters the *qi* of the whole body, and the heart is responsible for the blood. Blood and *qi* are just another expression of the whole vitality. We can ask why is the blood, which is liquid, linked to the heart which is *yang*? And why is the *qi*, which is an expression of *yang* nature, linked to the female lung? One can say two things about this. The first is that there is a crossing over as the *yin* becomes *yang* and the *yang* becomes *yin*. For example, in a Chinese legend about the creation of the world with Fuxi and Nügua, in classical times Fuxi was represented as a man and Nügua as a woman. The man, Fuxi, held in his hand a setsquare which represented earth, and Nügua held a compass which represented the circle and heaven. There has to be an exchange of powers so that there can be fertilization. This is seen at the moment of the birth of the world, and the same thing has to occur at each moment for the renewal of life in an individual. The examples of this are infinite.

Claude Larre: One more example is that the normal sequence in Chinese texts is heaven/earth and *yin*/*yang*. Heaven is the masculine principle, earth the feminine principle, but *yin* as the leading female in the second principle and *yang* as the following male principle. This is the way to contradict what has been said in order to link it for life.

Elisabeth Rochat: Another thing must be mentioned here. Blood is not only a liquid made of choice juices, it has passed through the heart. Liquid which has not passed through the heart is not called blood. The juices which are made in the middle heater by the stomach are very choice and rich. They are presented to the lungs by the spleen and oxygenation takes place there. Then they go to the heart. At that moment, says the Ling shu, there is a transformation which ensures that it actually becomes red from that point on, and this is the blood which then carries life to the whole body. So this liquid which is rich and full of life, penetrated by the power of the lungs, is also charged with the power and spirit of the heart, and it is because of this that the blood is red. It unites this quality of being a liquid with the colour of fire and life.

Claude Larre: To swear brotherhood people cut their veins, take some blood and mix it. This is done because it is intended that that which is mixed is not only a fluid but the spirits which are an essential part of the fluid. Something is done, not just symbolically but actually.

Elisabeth Rochat: Thus the blood, which some texts call the dwelling-place or residence of the spirits, has a very eminent position with regard to the *qi*. They have an equal position, and equal value. They cannot be separated. You have to have both for the maintenance and provision of life. The texts say they are like the body and its shadow. This marks the totality of a united couple, the heart and lung, together. When the lung fulfils its office of minister and chancellor well, what results from this is the regulation of all rhythms, *zhi jie* (治 節). In

Chinese zhi is to know how to live life. It can also mean to govern the kingdom, and if you know how to govern, you know how things operate, and how to regulate the whole thing.

Claude Larre: We may add a political statement, saying that the king has to maintain and to conserve. He may expand his territory, or the richness of the nation, but only up to a certain point, just as a man should not develop himself in order to have a big belly. There are limits. To govern is to govern life at the level of the empire or kingdom, at the level of the family, or at the level of the individual self. If you want more money maybe it is because you think the family will have a better life, but to raise this money means you are never at home. Then the family is destroyed just when you think you are building it up. It is the same for the emperor. He may extend his territory, and make war or peace to gain some advantage. But he is not the only one doing that and perhaps after so much warfare the nation will be exhausted, no men, no money, nothing. Afterwards the next king will be unable to recover from what his father has done.

Elisabeth Rochat: All this is at the level of the empire. When this character *zhi* (治) relates to the body it means to treat, cure or heal. It means that you understand the care that has to be taken either of the empire, or of your family, or of the body, or of yourself. There are two other characters made with the right hand part (台): with the flesh radical on the left it means embryo, *tai* (胎), and with the radical for woman on the left it means to begin, *shi* (始). In the text that we have here the radical on the left represents water, so there is something that is being constructed or built from a beginning. With someone who knows how to let life flow in conformity with the beginning you reach the meaning of to govern, to treat, to heal or to cure. With the character for life added afterwards you also have the popular expression for earning a living, *zhi sheng* (治 生).

Claude Larre: To earn a living you have to be clever enough to govern all circumstances in order to find a way to survive. Everywhere that this character *zhi* (治) is seen there is some sort of establishment, whether it is controlled by order or is something related to the body or to a woman, in all cases there is something which has to be maintained. This is the very profound feeling of the Chinese.

Elisabeth Rochat: So there is in the lungs a force which instinctively knows how to govern life, which perhaps makes us think of the *po* (魄), the soul.

The second character which shows the function of the lung, *jie* (節) is a knot of bamboo. The upper part of the character represents bamboo. What is interesting about bamboo is that it is the knots which mark its vitality. The distance or space between them marks the vitality of life. How the bamboo grows is shown by the knots, and as the years go by you can see it reflected in them. Bamboo is hollow, but where there is a knot there is a sort of concentration of life force, and it is just at this point, where the communication seems to be obstructed, that it is actually the most intense, since the knot permits the surging or production of a new section of bamboo. The Chinese love bamboo!

THE LIVER

肝

gan zhe jiang jun zhi guan
mou lü chu yan

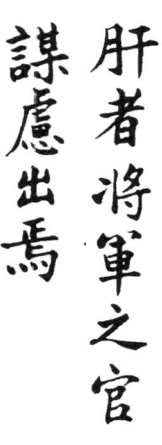

肝者將軍之官
謀慮出焉

The liver holds the office of general of the armed forces
Assessment of circumstances and conception of plans
stem from it

Claude Larre: Each of the *zang* is expressed by characters upon which we have to ponder in order to see, not exactly the translation, but the manifestation within it which is then developed in the sentence as the charge of the specific organ. This is the only way to go deeper than the ordinary level at which things are represented in our mind, and to simultaneously try and place our vision at the same starting point that the Chinese would naturally have devised and transmitted during their own teaching. To understand the etymology of a character gives the first enlightenment, and everything else takes place in that first light.

The second character in this sentence, *zhe*, (者) is the same for each of the *zang fu* presented: *xin zhe* (心 者), *fei zhe* (肺 者), *gan zhe* (肝 者), *dan zhe* (膽 者) *tan zhong zhe* (膻 中 者) and so on. It has the function of substantiating, or giving more importance to the preceeding word. It gives more insistence to this liver that we are now talking about, so usually it announces more elaboration around the subject of a sentence. If I say *gan* (肝), liver, as the ordinary beginning of an ordinary sentence it is not a statement as such. But *gan zhe* means beware, pay attention to this liver. This is not the only use of this character but it is the main one.

Jiang (將) is a strong hand. *Jiang* is really the man who is strong and who must be seen to be strong in order to impress the people. The general of the army, or the commander-in-chief has to be seen as a strong man. The fourth character, *jun* (軍),

is part of a character which we saw previously in *tian yun* (天運) when we were alluding to the celestial movement and to how everything goes in a perfect circle with the influences from heaven being regularly distributed to all creatures. This is *yun* (運), and the character is made by *jun* (軍) with the radical meaning to go, to march or to travel. *Jun* (軍) itself is made with a specific part of a chariot. Since there was no army in ancient times without a lot of chariots for the transportation of heavy arms, equipment and provisions, so a chariot, to the Chinese mind, always called up the idea of an army itself.

Guan (官) is the charge, being the representation under a roof of the buildings or places where administration takes place, and where everything is connected, making the offices efficient for the emperor. *Guan* has a different meaning from *chen* (臣) which we saw earlier when explaining the character of *zang*. We saw that inside the character of *zang* stands the small figure of a slave who became a servant to the emperor, and ascended to the dignity of a minister, maybe even prime minister. *Guan* is more the function and *chen* is more the person. So a *chen* has a *guan* as a servant has an office. When we say there are twelve *zang*, we may at the same time say that there are twelve charges. If we are speaking of *zang* we are speaking of the efficiency of life in a person, but if we are speaking of the twelve charges we are rather explaining how the functions of life are interconnected.

Mou lü chu yan (謀 慮 出 焉). *Mou* (謀) has the speech radical (number 149 言), not fluent speech, but speech as in a command or statement. Classical Chinese has the dignity of administration, of a court and so on, and since it is always dealing with heaven and earth the nobility of the universe is reflected in it. The speech aspect of *mou* is seen in the mouth which is the bottom part (口). On top is a sign of multiplication, that is multiplication of the emissions from the mouth. This is speech. *Lü* (慮) is made with the tiger radical. Inside and below one grouping of strokes has something to do with meditation, not spiritual meditation but the consideration of things of the past, or circumstances, or the situation in which you are. This part by itself is *si* (思), to think. Put inside the tiger radical it has increased vigour, and is the strength of the thought when it turns towards speculation. To speculate about something is to take normal thinking and go further and further, in order that the plan for operating something is ready before the operation itself.

The last important character is *chu* (出). *Chu* means to bring forth, to come out, to come out from the earth, or ground like a herb or any small little blade of vegetation emerging and being visible. What is done in the *zang* itself cannot really be seen except through the elaboration of the *qi* or the elaboration of the senses nourished by the *qi*. Due to the pressure of life, what is in the liver will later on show itself in the form of *mou* (謀) and *lü* (慮). All this chapter is constructed with the same systematic presentation. First there is the name of the *zang*, reinforced by the addition of *zhe* (者). Then the function is stated, and described as a *guan* (官). For example, the liver's function has something to do with or is exactly the same as the functions which are described as the duties and powers of the commander-in-chief of the army. So there is no description in terms of colour, biological function, connection with blood and so on, all that is not the scope of this chapter. The scope of this chapter is determined by the place of the chapter in the whole series of chapters, so number eight necessarily takes on the consideration of the highest level, where all the functions have their co-operation without any manifestation of illness or pathology. It is seen at the level of eight, which is the level of winds, the winds which are the moving of heavenly influx. It is somewhat like Genesis where the spirit of God was floating over the waters. At that level life is already on the way to organizing itself.

I left the character *gan* (肝) until last on purpose. It is better to have a framework for the consideration of the liver before looking at the image itself. The character *gan* has the flesh or part of the body radical (number 130 月) on the left side. Let me remind you that only the heart and triple heater do not have this radical, and the explanation for this which we saw earlier was that the heart is not part of the body as such, it is invisible, and the triple heater has no form and no visibility either. On the right side of the liver is the so-called phonetic with the sound of *gan* (干) (cf. Wieger Lesson 102 A). It represents a pestle, and by extension means to grind, or to destroy. At the same time it has the meaning of to oppose, to offend against, blunt arms, offence, or injury. We see that the upper part is like the horns of an ox, and that there is a stroke going downwards with a horizontal part to sustain that. So this device is strong enough to penetrate the ground or is good enough to grind cereals in a mortar. The feeling of the character is one of force, resistance, of offence, or of an appearance of life in which the demonstration of force is of the essence. It is quite different from what we saw with the heart. The heart is so peaceful, and is powerful by virtue of its own position, being at the centre and without visibility. The heart maintains things by itself without any demonstration of anything. But at the same time if there was not somebody to care for everything at the side of the sovereign then it would count for nothing. It would be like being the head of the Holy German Empire. Do you remember that? After the fall of Charlemagne everything fell into disorder, but the idea of a Germanic-Roman Empire was in the mind of the people, and they continued their national history under the guise of being related to this empire. It is also like the Zhou dynasty, when after a period of flourishing in the 8th century they had to move their capital because they were not very strong and the vassal kingdoms were no longer obedient and were just paying lip-service to the emperor. The dignity of the emperor was thus preserved, but he had no means of exerting any power. Thus the heart without the lung is a sovereign without any possibility of conducting the affairs of life. But to conduct the affairs of life with vigour is not the same as making a demonstration of strength. A demonstration of strength relies on another person, the commander of the army. The commander of the army will resist any attack from the barbarians, and if necessary will resist any upsurge from the citizens. Here we have clearly stated the function, or charge of the liver, and it is demonstrated in the character itself.

Elisabeth Rochat: The character *gan* (干) is the same as in the heavenly stems, *tian gan* (天 干), because it is a force or power which has a vertical axis, like a power coming down from heaven. It contrasts with the power that spreads out horizontally, which is more in line with the terrestial branches.

Claude Larre: You can see then that the stems and branches are not a construction of the mind which is unrelated to the duties of the liver. They apply to all the organs since there is a correlation between ten and twelve, or between two pairs of five and two pairs of six. Elisabeth says that when we say or write ten stems and twelve branches we put them in pairs, and this is done in order to correspond with the five elements and with the organization of the succession of time. Succession of time is not the measure of time, but the succession of influences which make time as energy or *qi*. Remember that we are always fighting against the measurement in our mind to liberate the thing which is being measured!

So, to come back to the liver, we say that it has the charge of being commander of the army. It means that it is for the defence of life, and something of an aggressive power is seen in the liver, something is springing up, and that is the reason why liver is spring. We do not say that liver is compared to spring, we say that liver is spring. Then we can understand that any vegetation or organic life which is a sort of plant is of the same quality as the liver. We say that the colour green is proper to plants and is proper to liver, and is also the colour for the spirits.

Many roofs on pagodas, small pavillions and temples necessarily have green glazed tiles since they are the manifestation of the presence of spirits. Reading chapters 4 and 5 of the Su wen we can see what is said about east, and we find that the eastern quarter is the first consideration of something separate from the oneness of *qi*. *Qi* in itself is indistinct, and we saw earlier that from one we come to two and from two to three and from three to four. When we come to four, within the oneness in our mind which reflects what is between heaven and earth, a quarter of what is really there is called east. If we look at the character for east we see a tree, and we see the power of life working in that tree as a sun. Thus we understand graphically that the east is the source of the power of liver. If somebody asks a question about the liver we have to consider its origin and state which quarter the liver is related to. If you know that it is the east then that is where you start your answer. All determinations on the same level will therefore have something to do with liver. Everything is reciprocal with everything else in this presentation of life.

Coming back to the charge, this is not easily defined for me. We saw that for heart and for lung there were two characters. With the heart there was the position, the sovereign or lord, and the expression, the mastering. With the lung we similarly had the position as minister close to the heart, and also that it is an auxiliary, giving an efficiency to the silent power of the heart, and the regulator of all the synapses of life. Now the question is, if I am using two Chinese characters to make a single French or English expression, commander of the army, why should we also not have two sides of the function, one the being of something, and the other the expression of that something? My feeling is that *jiang* (將) is the strength of the commander in himself, without any enforcement, and being strong, or pretending to be strong, since the pretending is in the character. Then *jun* (軍) is the way to make this power felt to enemies.

Elisabeth Rochat: It is just like we had in the heart. You have an aspect which is more heavenly, and a second aspect which is more earthly. In Chinese *jiang jun* (將 軍) is an expression of two characters that go together, they form a couple. *Jiang* (將) on its own has the sense of a general, of someone who is on the point of doing something, somebody who is ready and has got together all his capacity in order to make an action or do something. In current Chinese *jiang* (將) is often used to mark the future as in 'shall' or 'will'.

Claude Larre: Elisabeth rightly says that it is the idea of something which shall happen, or to be on the verge of doing something. That means that the preparation is already made, and the decision has already been taken, but that the execution is not yet under way. The action will be represented in the following character, *jun* (軍). The commander of the army who will move is *jiang jun* (將 軍). For there is no heaven without earth, and earth by itself is not able to do anything. It has to wait for the power coming from above which is inspiration without form. The difficulty for us in understanding heaven contrasted with earth is our difficulty in penetrating the logic of the Chinese mind, where heaven is nothing without earth but must be expressed as heaven. So we have to make some sort of statement saying that heaven is the initiative. But if you ask what sort of initiative, we have to call on earth in order to have a representation or formalization of this power. In books people usually do not pay enough attention and when they say that heaven is initiative, they want to say more and they use words which are taken from the role of earth, and these are inserted in the explanation without any warning. So finally you are never able to understand what the power proper to heaven is since just to express that power you need so many qualifications coming from the side of earth.

Elisabeth Rochat: The liver is the general of the armed forces. He has to be someone who is courageous, brave, and even impetuous, but that is only if it follows reflection beforehand. If not, that is the best way to lose the war! If we look at the The Art of War, the treatise by Sun zi from the 4th century BC, we find the following advice. If the general of the opposing army can easily be brought to anger, then do everything you can to anger him, and at that moment his mind will be all over the place. He will not see clearly anymore and he will direct his army without a good plan. You find here the emotion which is usually linked to the liver, *nu* (怒), anger. Anger is fundamentally an impetuous thrust that pushes life upwards. In fact the Chinese character is not always translated as anger, it can just be the effort to make things rise.

Claude Larre: A violent effort. For the Chinese and Japanese any sort of martial art has something to do with containing strength and liberating strength. The shouting is not intended to terrify the adversary, it is just to let the *qi* come out. And when you are doing that you are just acting along the lines of *nu* (怒).

Question: Does it have the heart radical underneath it?

Claude Larre: Yes, nearly all the sentiments are written with the heart underneath.

Elisabeth Rochat: *Nu* (怒) is the effort especially present at the beginning of doing something. But you have to be careful that it does not transform itself or change into anger which will scatter the spirits. It is for this reason that the general has to be careful to keep the balance between peace and war. He does not act the same way in times of peace as in times of war. In the same way the liver must keep the balance between its *yin* aspect of taking care of the blood that it stores, and the *qi* that it emanates. Similarly the liver has a different role with the blood depending on whether it is at rest or in activity. It is the liver that sends the blood to all the different parts of the body when the body is in movement, and in the same way it stores the blood and gathers it towards itself when it is not needed by the muscles. It is a similar, though completely different, rhythm to that of the lungs. With the liver it is a voluntary movement or rhythm which depends on the intensity of the movement or the depths of the rest. This gives a connection with the conception of plans and the assessment of circumstances. There is in the liver something that always has to estimate and evaluate the situation, whether it is for the quantity of blood available, for the fight against the perverse evils, or more generally for the conduct of mental or emotional life. This leads us quite naturally to the *hun* (魂) which are kept by the liver. Their role is to have this intelligence which allows evaluation and judgement, all of which you see in the liver.

When we say beginnings we also have to be clear about what we mean. We can have several kinds of beginnings. For example, with a plant does it begin when it comes up above the ground or when it comes out of the seed? What happens underneath the ground when the seed germinates is much more in the sphere of the kidneys. So there is a maintaining force, a basic force, which allows the appearance of the first signs of life and ensures that life does not die, and there is another force that allows life to surge up and appear.

Claude Larre: We come back to the old issue that the Chinese see the movements of life with a minute attention to detail. They are able to make distinctions between the power which keeps life and the power which allows development of the situation, when what is needed is not containment but a firm grasping in order to let it come forth or rush out. This is the reason why Elisabeth is making distinctions in the movement of life relating the first step to the kidneys where the maintaining is of the essence. Then, when it is no longer a question of keeping, we are at the end of winter and the beginning of spring. But where is the distinction inside life itself between winter and spring behaviour? That is the secret of life.

If you cast your vision in the direction of the past, then winter is more and more important, and if you evolve your imagination of life towards development, then spring is more and more influential. This is true at the change of each season, when the disturbances of the atmospheric conditions are in contradiction with the normal constitution of all beings. For example, if an organism is waiting for spring and the winter is too long and too severe, then if the reserves of the plant are not enough it has to die. Similarly if the heat is too much in summer then the plant dries up. What we see in the life of plants in gardening is the same in ourselves. It is important to know which organ is concerned when a problem arises due to a personal condition which is withstanding pressure and a general surrounding condition which is exerting a pressure. We have to see the role of the liver within the different variations of the conditions of life, such as the atmospheric conditions which are the subject of chapter 2. And the relation of one chapter to another has to be kept in mind. Here we are in chapter 8 but we have to refer to the commanding chapter which is chapter 2.

Elisabeth Rochat: The general of the armed forces is the one who spreads the influence of the empire everywhere in times of conquest, who has a masculine and impetuous force, and who has the same ability to penetrate physically as well as with thought. This ability to penetrate is like penetrating the future in order to make a plan, to make things circulate and unblock passages. You find this action of penetration or unblocking in many of the chapters on the pathology of the liver, especially in the knotting of *qi* due to a bad mental state, or in blood stagnation. And when the liver is carried away by anger you have the fire that rises up, like an army or troops that penetrate a different part of the country creating disorder.

Claude Larre: The final condition of that is that the troops themselves will be destroyed. You invade the territory of your neighbour and at first it is a big success. But finally you have exhausted all your own forces, you are far from your capital, your people and your sustaining basis. Then you will be destroyed there.

Elisabeth Rochat: This is just an an example of how you can in fact draw all the major pathology of the organs from chapter 8. One last thought is that the liver has the ability to consider and reflect, and at the same time has the courage of the general of the army. He is responsible for the muscles, not in the sense of flesh but in the sense of the activating force in the body, and the characteristic of the muscles in Chinese is to be like bamboo, supple and flexible. They must be able to go in a certain direction without getting blocked or obstructed, and be able to bend depending on the situation, just as the general with his battle strategy has to decide how to act according to the circumstances.

THE GALLBLADDER

膽

dan zhe zhong zheng zhi guan
jue duan chu yan

膽者中正之官
決斷出焉

The gallbladder is responsible for what is just and exact
Determination and decision stem from it

Claude Larre: From liver we move right on to the gallbladder. The character for gallbladder will be seen at the end of the explanation, as was the case with the liver. It is quite an elaborate character, but when it has been explained according to the etymology it will be found full of meaning, and not difficult to understand.

The gallbladder has something to do with the round, *zhong* (中), and the square, *zheng* (正). When something is not round it is square, and when something is not square it is round, because there is only heaven and earth. Heaven is round like your head and earth is square like your foot. Mankind is only the representation of heaven and earth at the level of his morphology, and at the level of his inspiration. It is too simple to say that the head is round and the foot is square, and besides some people may dispute that. So further explanation of what is round and what is square is needed.

What is round has no form. What is round is something very similar to what we call time. Time is circling, time has no form, time is close to heaven. But time without space, circle without square, does not work for mankind, because man, being at the junction or crossing of heaven and earth and being the response of earth to the solicitation of heaven, must have marked in himself the characteristics of round and square. As for the squareness of the foot one may observe that the ancient graphic really gave the impression of the square foot because all the toes are blocked and are more or less equal length. If you look at early Chinese inscriptions in bronze you really do have the feeling that they had the impression that the square was the way to express how man has contact with earth. Anybody who has seen Chinese architecture is convinced that everything is square or round. Square is the basis for all construction, but square does not necessarily mean a geometrical square. Square means that there is a 90 degree angle.

So we can assume that the expressions square and round mean that essentially there is something circling and perfect in roundness which is representative of heaven, and that the solidity, firmness and clarity of earth comes from the fact that it is regulated by the square. Whenever something is said in Chinese we have to make some sort of appreciation of it and some understanding of the two opposites. Heaven is more round than anything because of earth, and earth is more square than anything because earth is not heaven. One is the opposite of the other, and when you are not saying something, you are, in some other part of your mind contemplating what you are not saying. The person you are addressing hears what you have to say and also tries to hear what you are not saying. That is the Chinese way.

So we are not surprised here to see that the gallbladder is responsible for forms, not at the morphological level, but at the innermost level which is where life takes place and takes command. It is up to the gallbladder to be sure that your imaginative power and your strength, which have been shown in the liver, now come to a decisive step. And if you are supposed to take decisions, you have to take decisions that are absolutely exact. They are exact when they are in the middle, and they are exact when they are correct. *Zhong* (中) has the meaning of an arrow sent to the target and hitting it right in the middle so that you see the arrow cutting it in two. So one part of being exact is to hit the mark. This reflects the heavenly side of all propositions, all problems and all decisions. They have to be exact.

We also say we have to be just. When you are looking over students' papers for marking you have to be just in your mind. It is not a question of being kind or benevolent, it is a question of your own mind being right. Our relationship with Chinese people shows us that fancy does not alter judgement. They are usually very exact and correct. It is some sort of quality which is in the civilization, and is inscribed and reflected in the classical texts. There is never hesitation. It is true or it is false, just or not, exact or not. This sort of dogmatism sets the Chinese free. It lets them make any fanciful construction they wish to build - palaces for fairies in the air, spirits going here and there, all the festivals, all the tales of the imagination and so on. It is very colourful! But when it comes to things which have to be decided upon they have the same sort of spirit as our own engineers building a machine, you take measurements and you produce exactly what is wanted. Who is responsible for that? The gallbladder. The gallbladder comes with the liver and makes some sort of formalization of the energy, and gives the plan its correctness. So we can see the very close association between liver and gallbladder.

Where do we see more precisely the effect of it being round and square, correct and exact? We see it in the decision. The power is in the gallbladder but the decision is the effect of that power. Decision is expressed by two characters, one is *jue* (决) and the other is *duan*. There is the same mutual relationship between these two characters as we saw in the cases of heart, lung and liver, and in the others to come since there is always an expression formed by two characters. *Jue* (决) has the water radical on the left, and *duan* (斷) has an axe on the right side.

Elisabeth Rochat: In *jue* (决) there is the idea of a decision taken. There is the idea of forcing a passage. Whether it is a decision or a circulation everything has to be done with natural upsurge. What has this ability to force a passage or a decision is on the side of the *yang*, and within the *yang* it is *shao yang* (少 陽), the young *yang* full of force and some kind of promise for the future. You can see in chapter 8 in the definition of the twelve charges that there are very few characters that are repeated, but this character *jue* (决) comes again in the description of the charge of the triple heater, which is the other *shao yang*. In the case of the function of the triple heater it is linked to the idea of making everything, all the *qi* and the liquids that are carried by the *qi*, circulate correctly so that nothing can obstruct or block the circulation. So *jue* (决) gives the idea of something that makes its way, makes a channel, because it is deeply anchored in a decision that has been taken. *Jue* (决) is profoundly anchored and has the force of passing all obstructions and obstacles.

The other character, *duan* (断), is the image of an axe. This shows it is something clean-cut. This function is reaffirmed in the next chapter of the Su wen, chapter 9, when it is said that the eleven viscera come to the gallbladder to make the decisions.

Claude Larre: It means they are not able to make a decision by themselves, so they go to the gallbladder. This is like two people who are quarrelling with one another and are not able to make a decision, they go to court, and the court clearly cuts through the problem saying you are right, you are wrong, you are partially right, you are partially wrong, you owe so much money and so on. When we come to the triple heater we will come back to the question of why they use *jue* (决) twice.

Elisabeth Rochat: But there is a question which has to be answered. Why is such an important charge given to one of the *fu*? And also why does the gallbladder come in the fourth position before the other two *zang*?

First we must see that the function of the gallbladder is the logical continuation of the liver. Liver and gallbladder are a couple, a very close-knit couple both in medical terminology and in popular use.

Claude Larre: Let me refer you to Zhuang zi chapter 2. The discussion there is whether the liver and gallbladder are very much united or very much separate from one another. It is not exactly put as a question but as an observation that if you want to see how they are similar you may say that there are no two things more closely related than gallbladder and liver. In Zhuang zi, which is certainly not a typical medical work, they use a popular expression saying they are like the fingers of a hand. But, they say, if you are looking from the point of view of some sort of inner difference you see that there are no two things more separate than gallbladder and liver because one is a *zang* and one is a *fu*. The same thing seen from different angles is either very close or very much apart.

Elisabeth Rochat: The liver analyses or assesses circumstances and decides the plan of action. The gallbladder, being a *yang* aspect of the liver will have the firmness to make a clean decision and force through the situation so that the decision can be carried out, spreading the orders of the general far and wide. The gallbladder is the *shao yang* (少 陽) or young *yang*, which gives the force or strength of the beginning of life, just like the spring. The first month of the year is often called *zheng yue* (正 月). *Yue* (月) means month and *zheng* (正) is the same character that we find here meaning correct. Why is this? Because it is in the beginnings and the first appearances of something that we have to follow a good line. If, when a tree springs up from the ground, it is knocked sideways or bent by the wind or by storms then it will grow that way, bent. It is the same force that makes things spring upwards which also assures some kind of rectitude and straight growth.

This power of beginnings is linked in another way to the origins of life since we know that the *shao yang* is very much connected to the fire of *ming men* (命 門). This is particularly the case with the triple heater which commands all the *qi* of the body, assuring the renewal and circulation of all *qi* from posterior heaven, and ensuring the circulation in the body of all *qi* from the original *qi*. The *shao yang* has a close relationship to and is rooted in the original *qi* of *ming men* and the depths of the being. It is because of this that it has the extreme force to take the right direction in life. It is life springing up, like fire that springs out of water, just as the liver and gallbladder come after the kidneys and bladder.

The direction of life depends on its own deep nature. All that goes in a direction other than the proper direction for life will create difficulty. It is therefore in the root of your life that you should find a good direction, and it is in *ming men* (命 門) or the *qi* of *ming men* that the root of your life is found under the name of original *qi*, *yuan qi*, of authentic *yin* and *yang* or original, authentic fire and water. When we use the word authentic it means something that conforms to the real, deep nature of an individual. Now we know that *shao yang* has a privileged place in relation to the original *qi* which is particularly expressed by the triple heater, whose main function is to make *qi* circulate and diffuse according to the model given by the original *qi*, yuan *qi* (元 氣). The gallbladder also has the same quality of *shao yang* which gives it the capacity to give good direction to things in life. It is because of this that it governs the first aspects and the beginnings of things. For this reason all the other organs come to the gallbladder in order to have it make decisions.

There is another important aspect concerning the gallbladder which is that it is not an ordinary *fu* (府). It is an extraordinary *fu*. In Chinese it is *qi heng zhi fu* (奇 恆 之 府). *Fu* (府) is *fu* and *zhi* (之) is a connective particle. *Qi* (奇) is something out of the ordinary, something extraordinary. This means that it is something different from the normal everyday conduct of life. *Heng* (恆) is something that is a continuity, some kind of equilibrium. It is a permanent equilibrium, something very stable. When we have this expression *qi heng* it is not referring to something that is very extraordinary or magical, something fabulous or fantastic, it is just showing the regulation of life beyond the ordinary functioning. But it is a regulation which is not visible because it is much deeper, and it is deeper because it was there before other regulations, just as the eight extraordinary meridians (which have the same character *qi* 奇) are a regulation before, below or at a deeper level than the twelve meridians.

So here we have the *qi heng zhi fu*, the extraordinary *fu*, at the level of the beginning of the being. These are the *fu* which are special because they store, and what they store are, of course, the essences. The normal *fu* are especially concerned with the digestive function, but they do not keep hold of anything. They make things circulate, evacuate, come in and go out. The storage of the essences is the function of the *zang*. The extraordinary *fu* therefore have the name of *fu* because they do not store for the spirits but they store the essences, *jing* (精), to make the body work, and to give the body good form. It is for this reason that in Su wen chapter 11 they are given a definite relationship with the *qi* of the earth. In the present chapter, chapter 8, we are at the fourth charge, the fourth official, and four is a number which is linked with the *qi* of the earth, for the distribution and spreading out which is well-ordered and well-conceived. This goes with the function of the gallbladder, governing in a certain way its distribution and construction. On the other hand there is the fact that the gallbladder stores the essences, which gives it a place not exactly amongst the *zang*, but an elevated position because it works on that which is clear, and not on that which is cloudy, impure and un-clear.

What is clear, *qing* (清), is something which is so pure that it rises and diffuses in the same way as the *qi* that constitute heaven. You can see in the characters for essences and clear, *jing* (精) and *qing* (清), that there is a common element. This part, which is pronounced *qing* (青), is often called the colour green, or blue-green. It is in fact the colour of life. It is the aspect that is seen in beings when they are full of life. For example, in springtime, when the sap that is full of life rises upwards, then the vegetation in the fields has this colour *qing*.

And you can look at the sky and say that it has the same colour because the sky or heaven is full of invisible life. The Chinese also said that the poet Li Po, who was one of the greatest poets of the Tang dynasty in the 8th century AD, had green hair! This does not mean that he was like the punks in London and Paris, it just means that he manifested an exceptional quality of virtue in his poems. It means that his *qi* had an extraordinary quality, rising from his kidneys up to his head. His blood was full of life rising to the top of his head, so that the 'vegetation' growing there revealed his deep vitality, making his hair a beautiful shining black. But what is called black here is this same character *qing* (青), which means not green, but to be manifesting a deep vitality.

What we call essence, *jing* (精), is everything that is good for the renewal of this vitality, which can be drawn from seeds and cereals, and what we call clear, *qing* (清), is the movement of this animation of life which is given by the flux of liquids and vapours. This gives the idea of rising to heaven and of circulating and diffusing. That which is not-clear will have a movement of condensation and lowering. In the case of digestion that which is clear is extracted from food to be incorporated into my being or vitality, and that which is not-clear goes downwards through the digestive organs, the stomach, small intestine, large intestine and bladder, and will finish by being evacuated as excrement or urine.

Claude Larre: We should come back to the very important

question of why the correctness and the right direction of life is connected through the *shao yang* (少 陽) to the original *qi*, *yuan qi* (元 氣), and to the *qi* in the sphere of posterior heaven. Why does *shao yang* have this directness and firmness that enables it to give the right direction to life, and why does this have a special relationship with the *yuan qi*? Let me just return to what we were saying about archery. To hit the mark the arrow must fly in the right direction, but it must previously have been held in the most stable position on the bow itself, held firmly between two or three fingers in the hand of the archer. But this hand is itself firmly at the end of the arm, and the arm is connected with the stability of the trunk. The stability of the trunk is given by the mind and the breath, and if the breathing is not correct or the mind not peaceful, and if the eye is not in a position to see the relationship of the tip of the arrow with the target, then there may be some deviation. So we can see that the correctness, and the straightness of shooting the arrow is based in the most profound origin of life in the archer, and we know that *shao yang* has something very close to this quality of the fired arrow. *Shao yang* is not, as is very often translated, a lesser *yang*, it is young *yang*.

Question: Does the character *shao* (少) in *shao yang* (少 陽) give any idea of it being a hinge, as for example in the penetration of fevers where you have *shao yang* as the last *yang* stage from where it could possibly go deeper into the *yin* stage or back to *yang ming* (陽 明)? As I understand it, the character implies the channelling in one direction, like a river flowing in one direction, and you pointed out its clarity of direction, while the hinge is more of a mechanical idea of going either way.

Claude Larre: It may be contradictory in your mind, but when a man is firmly established in a place with a clear vision of something, he may suddenly turn the other way. This is just because he is in that position of command. It is typically Chinese to be able to keep in mind the two necessarily reciprocal aspects of something. So this hinge effect you were alluding to is the complementary aspect of the firmness which is in the origin of the being.

Question: But the word hinge implies a mechanical action or force, and the character very much gives the feeling of energy flow, of dominating or regulating that.

Claude Larre: That's true! And furthermore one of the most important and difficult Chinese characters related to this is *ji* (機), which is a crossbow. A crossbow is a very small mechanism where the force and strength is kept tight before unleashing. *Ji* is in the expression *shi ji* (時 機), which means occasion, and the *ji* is the turning point of the occasion. For example, you had the chance to come to this seminar, and it may change your life! The occasion is a *ji* (機). The upper part is the silk character written twice, and on the left hand side is the wood radical which implies a mechanism because machines were built in wood not iron or metal then.

The difficulty with English or French words is that when we pay attention to the meaning we may be misled. We may think that there are twelve meridians, and that we call the further eight extra because we already have that supply of twelve. But that is very silly as a concept because we start with the eight, so which are the extra ones? It is the same with the *fu* (府). Which are the extraordinary ones? Because like the meridians the extraordinary *fu* are formative for life, they have to be quoted first and regarded as more important than the others. The whole field of acupuncture is full of these kinds of things which are not false but which have been presented without any systematization according to the old Chinese classical texts. What we are trying to do in all our teaching is to keep as much as possible to what has actually been written, and to place it in a larger picture where everything is just a component. And sometimes we have to comment on one presentation or one given name in order that everything fits together.

Elisabeth Rochat: If we take the order of presentation of the *zang* in the eighth chapter we see that the first three are the *zang* which have the function of storing the essences and of government by the spirits, and they they are linked to the three higher aspects which relate to the spirits, the *shen* (神), the *po* (魄) and the *hun* (魂). We also see that the gallbladder is linked to beginnings, to the essences and to the pure and clear. We see that the centre of the chest is located in the upper heater, and here we have a separation or a pivot, with the role of the stomach and spleen which are also concerned with the clear and not-clear. Then we come to the realm of the intestines which are concerned with what is not-clear.

Here we can see that the gallbladder is acting in its role as one of the extraordinary *fu* working on the essences and being full of clear, pure juices which it sends out to particularly help with digestion. You can also see that in the series of the first five officials, three functions relate to the upper heater, the region above the diaphragm, which itself protects them from everything rising up from the lower regions. We can see that it is a place from which the circulation of the breath begins, especially at *tan zhong* (膻 中), the sea of *qi* in the chest. And we have the liver and gallbladder which traditionally belong in the lower heater. This is not to say that they have an inferior position, but rather that they manifest the vitality of life from the depths. It is because of this that the liver is in fact situated or located higher than the kidneys or the intestines. What is very striking to the Chinese is also the difference in size between the liver and the gallbladder. The liver expresses its power with a development of form, and the gallbladder by a concentration of force or strength.

Claude Larre: These spirits which are called *hun* (魂), stored in the liver, are responsible for the imaginative life. Nowadays, when there are new trends in science, it is important to be clear about imagination. Imagination leads to new discoveries and is a way to escape from the rigidity of either round or square. So doctors who study with us and who have had a strict teaching from the Occidental mind come because they feel that as good as their training and practice is, something is missing. Imagination is then the complement for any other exercise of the spirit in ourselves. But this does not mean that Chinese medicine is imaginative to the point of not being exact and correct. It is exact and correct in observation and has the logic of the living being in order to regulate these observations and allow them to fall into place and produce patterns.

As I have said before, Chinese paintings are closer to the natural state of things than photography. The photograph gives you the external appearance. But the limit of the external description is that it usually takes such a hold in the mind that there is no place left for the imaginative power. If we understand this relation of the imaginative power to the external vision, it leaves enough hope that the imaginative power will be regulated by some inner mystery of the universe and not just fanciful thinking. The imaginative power is necessary to displace the frontiers of knowledge itself, and this is proper to the liver, controlled by the decisions of the gallbladder.

Presently we will be talking about the regulation of mind which is proper to the spleen and kidneys. Then it will be appropriate to look again at the *shen* (神), the *hun* (魂), the *po* (魄), the *yi* (意) and the *zhi* (志), and to understand that the mental system is dominated by heart, lungs, liver and also the gallbladder, but could not really do without the inferior *zang* which are in a position of service. The will power and the power to make things in a form are subservient to the higher power. This appears illogical in the Occidental system of the functioning of the mind, which has to be above the body, though nobody knows what 'above' means exactly! But in the Chinese system we see that all that is essential to make a full image of mental life is distributed some at the highest level and some at the lowest level. Nothing in this scheme is by accident, and that is the reason why one has always to be on guard and not to overlook the way, the time, and the position, where and when things are said.

TAN ZHONG

膻中

tan zhong zhe chen shi zhi guan
xi le chu yan

膻中者臣使之官
喜樂出焉

Tan zhong has the charge of resident as well as envoy
Elation and joy stem from it

Claude Larre: *Tan zhong* (膻 中) is something we do not understand since it is not French or English, it is just pure Chinese, and there is no translation. It is necessary that we leave the two Chinese characters without a translation because there is no such thing as *tan zhong* in Occidental medicine.

The text runs: *Tan zhong zhe chen shi zhi guan xi le chu yan* (膻 中 者 臣 使 之 官 喜 樂 出 焉). The character *zhong* (中) has been seen already, and we know that it is not safe to just translate it as the middle! The translation of *zhong* has to be made specifically in each context. *Zhong* is so beautiful and so simple and much used as a character in Chinese, not only in medicine but everywhere in Chinese books. So we must pay special attention to the spiritual value of *zhong* and of its complementary character *nei* (內). *Nei* is the interior, and *zhong* (中) is the so-called middle, but the interior may not be internal, and *zhong* might not be the middle but just the position between two other things. So it is better not to rush into any translations for characters like *nei* and *zhong*. They do not have the same significance as other characters.

Chen (臣) was seen previously to be the slaves and servants who became ministers. It was found within the character *zang* (臟). *Chen* is a position, a trust, and the *chen* is more or less detained in the palace, he is under the jurisdiction of the court. *Shi* (使), on the other hand, are officials sent from the court to different countries with the status of ambassadors, or as representatives of different ranks. Or they could be just sent to deliver messages. So the opposition between *chen* and *shi* is the usual opposition we saw for all previous functions. The division is between the people who stay and work in one place as opposed to the people who are sent outside. To be sent outside means that they are a manifestation of the court, because the court is the inner life of China, and the ambassadors or people sent on missions, are manifestations of the power, glory and life-giving power of China. And China, an empire, a kingdom or the body are only different kinds of life in a state.

Xi le chu yan (喜 樂 出 焉). Here we are concerned with the specific production of *tan zhong*. If we look at the characters we see that the first, *xi* (喜), and the second, *le* (樂), have some similarity with *shen ming* (神 明). While we were talking of the heart as producing life under a certain aspect, we saw that this aspect of production was a state of spirituality and radiance. The heart gives this aura of spirituality to the face, the behaviour, the deportment and the language of the person. Now we see that *tan zhong* is giving something very close to that. When a young couple is about to get married the Chinese present them with a lot of gifts with these two characters, *xi* (喜) and *le*, (樂) on them, and New Year's cards are often inscribed with the *xi* (喜) character. *Xi* (喜) is a kind of excited joy, and *le* (樂) is when joy is calm and profound, silently pervading the heart. This is solid joy. So an excited joy and a solid joy are the product and the radiance proper to *tan zhong*.

In relation to *tan zhong* (膻 中) perhaps we might ask Roger if he could say something about *tian tan* (天 壇), the Temple of Heaven because the two *tan* characters are very similar.

Roger Hill: I would like to start off with a broad map of Beijing which is a walled city in origin, built on a very ancient site but developed at about the end of the 15th century. Slightly north of the centre is the Imperial Palace, which in itself is an architectural lesson on the structure of man, with the head, the kidneys and the heart. On the way in there is a stream over which there are five little bridges indicating the five senses, which in turn indicate the communion between the inner part of man and the outside world. The Temple of Heaven is in the south eastern quarter of this ancient city, and there is a relationship here between the imperial power as used to govern the empire, and the imperial power in relationship with heaven. This is expressed geographically as well as in terms of function.

The Temple of Heaven is also a walled enclave in its own right, a walled temple with gatekeepers and a huge park around the outside. The emperor would go there on two occasions in the year, the winter solstice and the autumn equinox I think, to perform ceremonies which would last the whole of one day. To give you some idea of the scale you should think in terms of Hyde Park for the size of the whole area. Within that the temple is divided into three parts. There is the circular temple with a long connecting causeway to another area which was walled off with a smaller temple in the middle, and then another causeway to three more open platforms.

So you have the central north-south axis, and three main units, of which the middle one is walled. The open platforms are in mathematical and architectural terms, an expression of the law of three. Their whole construction is based on the number three. You have three platforms rising up, and every architectural detail is a multiple of three, so that on the top platform there are eighty one paving stones radiating from the middle. The next platform down is a larger multiple by three of eighty one, and so on. Around each of these platforms is a balustrade made of marble which again reflects a multiple of three, the law of three, heaven, earth and man. One of the tricks in terms of sound in this part of the temple is that if you stand in the middle, where it is completely open, and you speak as if from a position of quietness, not only inner quietness but also external quietness, you will hear back an echo of your own voice, even though you speak apparently to the open air. It has a similar quality to the Taj Mahal in that respect, being a most perfect sounding box and returning to you the nature of your own expression.

The two temples are quite similar to each other. Like all Chinese buildings they are raised from the earth and in this case have a platform of three steps. The roof, supported on pillars, is always an important part of any Chinese building whether it is a humble domestic peasant dwelling, or a palace or temple like this. There are basically three roofing tile colours in China:

grey for ordinary use, yellow or golden for imperial use, and blue which is used to reflect the power of heaven and found only in great imperial temples such as this. You have a circular building supported by twelve massive columns on the outside representing the twelve months of the year, the twelve two-hour divisions of the day and so on. Inside are four pillars representing the number four with the implication of the fifth in the middle. It was to this crossing point in the northernmost temple, looking south down through the rest of the structure, that the emperor would come to give his obeisance and to pray for good harvests.

Claude Larre: Thank you Roger. From what has been said here about *tian tan* (天 壇) you can see that if *tan zhong* (膻 中) is related to that structure, everything which has been said here has a relevance for *tan zhong*. To make explicit the relationship we have to see which character is used for temple in the Temple of heaven, and which character is used for *tan* in *tan zhong* (膻 中). Also, if the comparison is good, the nobility of *zhong* (中) now appears in the context of heaven. Some people may object that if you are always pushing the interpretation towards heaven you will not understand the logic of Chinese thinking, but I think it is just the contrary. The more you push statements beyond a sensible appreciation the more you stay in the tradition given by the classical texts. It is a pity to see that some constriction of mind natural to the modern Occidental way of thinking now presses on the Chinese mind. There are few people either inside or outside China who can withstand the pressure which is making Chinese civilization turn around when it has been built the other way. So it is important not to accept any reduction of meaning when it is not clearly indicated in the text or context.

Looking at the two characters, if you take the *tan* of *tian tan* (天 壇) and replace the earth or humus radical on the left (土) with the flesh or part of the body radical (月), then you no longer have the Temple of Heaven but some sort of temple in man himself. The character (膻) which is pronounced *tan*, or sometimes *shan*, designates the central area of the chest. If the spirits are supposed to dwell somewhere they may well dwell in the heart, but they can also remain in *tan zhong* since there is a place for them at the point where the vital movement of life occurs and where excitement and profound joy are realised. So even when we do not know the meaning of *tan zhong* we take for granted that it is a place and a function since it has to be located somewhere. And when we are talking of the human body there must also be a place there for *tan zhong*.

We know the charge or function of *tan zhong* has been described as *chen shi* (臣 使). *Chen shi* may be just the opposite of *jun zhu* (君 主) which was the heart as lord and master, the lord by position and the master by destination or operation. Facing the lord there is the servant, and facing the master there are all those officials who are able to dispatch the executive power which characterize the master. From that perspective, without any knowledge of what *tan zhong* is, we know that it is facing the heart.

Elisabeth Rochat: First of all we have to consider *tan zhong* in this series of twelve charges. In this series we might expect to see the heart master, the heart governor or the pericardium, but none of these appear at all, and neither does the expression *xin bao luo* (心 包 絡) appear anywhere in the Su wen, nor the expression heart master (*xin zhu* 心 主).

Claude Larre: For that I require one minute of silence from the audience just to commemorate the death of *xin bao luo* (心 包 絡)! This is a very important fact. I am sure that on leaving this seminar you will resume your old habits and be sure that *xin bao luo* is really the twelfth *zang*, but you have to make a decision about that yourself!

Elisabeth Rochat: The character *zhong* (中) in *tan zhong* (膻 中) is the middle, the centre, the point from which an influence will spring up and radiate out. *Tan zhong* is also the name of the point Ren 17, the sea of *qi* in the chest. It is the place where the *zong qi* (宗 氣), the ancestral energy exists. What this means is that *tan zhong* is a place where there is an activity which we call ancestral *qi*. The texts do not describe a circulation of ancestral *qi*, since that is not what it means. What we call ancestral *qi* is, in effect, what is created in the middle of the chest, in the centre. It is there that everything which is going to have this effect is reunited or joined or gathered.

The middle heater contributes to this point with what is drawn from food and drink in order to renew the essences. There is also the contribution of the lower heater, the fire of *ming men* (命 門), that rises to the upper heater. There is also the *qi* which comes in through respiration, the proximity of the heart and the radiation of the spirits from the heart, and all this is joined here and creates what we call the sea of *qi* in this place where all the ancestral *qi* is accumulated and gathered together. The Chinese term which we are translating by accumulate is an accumulation which is not a piling up, it is an accumulation of virtue.

Claude Larre: It is an endless springing of virtue's well, it is not piling up as in storage. It wells up.

Elisabeth Rochat: This makes life function effectively. Ancestral *qi* is what makes the mechanism of inspiration and expiration in breathing. It is through the lungs that one breathes, but in order that the mechanism of inspiration and expiration takes place it is necessary to have this ancestral *qi*. It is because of this that the business of respiration in general is not just the duty of the upper heater but also of the middle and lower heaters, especially the kidneys.

Claude Larre: If I may interrupt for one moment, we come here to a point where Chinese thinking is quite different from what we have in our own ways of representing life. We say that it is not enough to just have the mechanism, we also have to provide the *zong qi* (宗 氣) in order to operate this mechanism. This comes from the fact that we are obliged to make a distinction between the mechanism and an operator, or having enough supply of fuel to make the machine work. But we have to remind ourselves that the machine is life itself. It is because we are not able to share the Chinese concept of life that we divide the mechanism of life, the operation, the operator and the fuel supply. It is the fact that we want to explain things which multiplies all these intermediaries.

Even if we are not looking at life, life is still there, and between life and life there is no mechanism, no operator and no fuel supply, since it is impossible to separate the operator from the machine, or the creation from the fuel supply needed to maintain the creation. It is our own reflective minds which oblige us to make so many distinctions. So in a way, when somebody outside the world of acupuncture listens to what we are saying they might think we are discussing the sex of angels! But we cannot do otherwise. The limits are set by the text. If the text does not say that there is an operator or an operation, then why should we say it? That would be criticising the way tradition expresses life, and who dares to do that? In certain places the tradition is very prolix, and in others is very brisk and dry, but when it is so implicit it is just because it is relying on more detailed explanation elsewhere. So we have to make a judgement about what we choose to explain, and to try and steer a middle course between too strict pronouncements and too much prolix explanation. We are not in a position to do anything other than follow the text.

Elisabeth Rochat: The ancestral *qi* that is at *tan zhong* makes respiration work and makes the *qi* circulate throughout the body, in particular the defensive and nutritive *qi* which have their point of departure in *tan zhong*.

Claude Larre: The meaning of this is that even though it comes from the three heaters the true place for its influence in the general circulation is in the chest.

Elisabeth Rochat: This *qi* goes everywhere, even to the most external parts of the body, the nails and the hair, and this makes one think of the function of the lungs to propagate, and diffuse the *qi*. This is different from the function of the lungs concerning the rhythm of circulation, here we have a movement of coming together like rivers that flow into the sea.

Claude Larre: Or like the sea accepting the rivers, you can see it both ways. A river flows to the sea or the sea, being lower, attracts the rivers just by its position.

Elisabeth Rochat: There is another very important function of the *zong qi* (宗 氣) which is to make the heart beat, and to give it the possibility of manifesting its life through its movement. It is thus that we see *tan zhong* is really serving the master and sovereign, giving him everything he needs to make the heart beat and the blood pulsate through the vital circulations, the *mai* (脈). This is also how *tan zhong* is the messenger going out like an ambassador or courier, ensuring that the orders of the heart are carried out everywhere. *Tan zhong* is at the origin of the circulation of *qi* and the movement of blood.

Within the series of chapter 8, *tan zhong* is in the fifth position. It is therefore the centre that gathers together and from which all these effects radiate out. It is different from the rhythm of the lungs which has the function of holding a morning audience with the *mai*. It is different from the energy of the liver which can penetrate any obstacle. It is also different from the *shen ming* (神 明), the subtle radiance of the spirits of the heart. Coming in the fifth position it is a kind of recapitulation, or résumé. It is because of this that *tan zhong* is a sea, and it is from here that all influences in the form of *qi* or blood go out into the body, just as at the moment of the winter solstice the emperor leaves his palace to go to the Temple of Heaven in order to create the harmony which has to last the whole year. It is precisely because he performs the rites there that the beneficial effect spreads out to the whole of his people, and this kind of influence is expressed in two characters, *xi* (喜) and *le* (樂), elation and profound joy. There has to be some kind of excitation so that the movement of breathing and beating can be made, and when it is made there is the sense that the whole body will be taken over with this excitement of life.

The other aspect is the deep sense of the joy of being alive and being in harmony with heaven. When one speaks of joy related to life or the power of heaven we use the character *le* (樂) which means music. Music is a very important part of Chinese classical civilization, coupled with the rites. Rituals give order, make separations and distinction. Everyone has their place and their rank in the hierarchy, and has to make certain movements or stay in certain positions during the ritual.

Claude Larre: I am going to add a casual remark! When you are invited to a restaurant by Chinese friends, ritual is necessary. When you arrive they will offer tea, even if there is no reason for it. They they will start talking about the weather and the general condition of life, and a lot of other talk. I know this is not a surprise for you because English people do the same! And as the ritual goes on you reach a point where things are very loose and no rite is observed any longer. But nearing the end you feel the ritual power coming back, and everybody knows that the time for leaving has come. This is the chaining or linking of life. Without all that it is impossible to have social life. But there is much that is boring, even for the Chinese, and something has to compensate for that, and that is music.

Elisabeth Rochat: Music links together and unites the hearts of all the people. People who have different positions and different movements in the ritual have to have something which will bring them together and create a unity, and this is the role of music. That is why in all the great Chinese rites you have the presence of music. The character *le* (樂) shows some kind of orchestra (cf. Wieger Lesson 88 C). But why does music create unity? It is because all music comes from the heart of man. This is a phrase which is repeated many times in the Book of

Rites. Music touches the heart of man and will touch all that is most deep and heavenly in his heart. In texts on music it is written that music makes the blood circulate correctly and makes the energy flow correctly in the *mai*.

Claude Larre: So when you go to a concert you feel that your mind has been refreshed and that you are ready for work and all that. But usually you do not count on it for the regulation of your own circulation of blood and spirits because we are inclined to separate the mind from all the movement proper to life and from all bodily functions. The Chinese, on the other hand, would say that music has this effect on blood or *qi* circulation. This is the difference in outlook.

Elisabeth Rochat: So *tan zhong* (膻 中), being the servant and messenger of the heart creates this free and easy circulation of everything which makes life and which is also the joy that belongs to life. Close to the heart it will maintain and sustain it, and far away from the heart it will allow the spirits to express and direct or control life. *Tan zhong* is like a kind of protection of the heart. In the Su wen it says that *tan zhong* is like the Forbidden City, the palace which surrounds and protects the sovereign. The agents who go on missions are just like the meridian of the heart in activity, *xin zhu* (心 主), which is the heart as master. If you are looking at it from the point of view of the *qi*, then *chen* (臣) is connected to the *zong qi* (宗 氣), and *shi* (使) is connected to the nutritive and defensive *qi*.

Claude Larre: I would just like to add that the meaning of *zhong* (中) is now clear. It is not the centre of *tan* (膻), it is *tan* acting as a centre, and it is constructed in the same pattern as we saw for *jun zhu* (君 主) or the other positions. The difference here is that for the first time we have a *zang* with a double name. From the very fact that it is not a single character, like *gan* (干) liver, *xin* (心) heart, or *fei* (肺) lung, but an expression in which we have to try to understand how the first character is playing with the other one, and vice-versa. The only explanation is that *tan* (膻) is really the specific indication, but how, where and why this specific indication is there, is found in *zhong* (中), to be the centre. When you occupy the centre you are the centre, and when it is no longer useful you should retire, as Lao zi says.

The usual translation for *zhong* is middle or centre, but here *zhong* is associated with *tan*. If we just make a translation for *zhong* and a translation for *tan* then the richness of the expression formed by their close union will be lost. That is always the case when two characters join to make an expression, and even more so when three characters do. This is seen clearly in *xin bao luo* (心 包 絡). We have to understand *xin* (心) and *bao* (包) and *luo* (絡) and *xin bao* (心 包) and *bao luo* (包 絡) and *xin luo* (心 絡) and *xin bao luo* (心 包 絡). That is the power of the classical expression in the characters. They are images and schemes. A character has an emblematic power, so it gives you not only a meaning in the mind, but a desire to do something.

Question: I would like to clarify the terms used for the different energies.

Peter Firebrace: Ancestral *qi* is *zong qi* (宗 氣), original *qi* is *yuan qi* (元 氣) and authentic *qi* is *zhen qi* (真 氣).

Claude Larre: I would say that from the point of view of the unique *qi* in the universe, which is always in yourself, it is dependent on the origin. Everybody is purely themselves in the origin. Everybody here is full of *yuan qi* (元 氣), and for that reason we are connected together, we have the same *qi* circulating here and there. But in terms of *zong qi* (宗 氣) each one of us has a special fate and a special, specific nature. So although the *yuan qi* is common it is not the same in each of us because the *zong qi* is not the same in each of us. In you the *yuan qi* and the *zong qi* are the same *qi* because your *yuan qi* informs all that you do in a way that is similar to the ancestral energies. And, as long as you practise respiration and nourishment, function with the seasons and so on, then you preserve what has been given to you. But what has been given, which is the virtue of heaven, is nothing other than the *zhen qi* (真 氣). They are all authentic, but concretely speaking all of them should be different.

Elisabeth Rochat: To say the same thing in other words: the original *qi*, the *yuan qi*, in me is what is called *qi* of anterior heaven, or pre-heaven. That is to say, it is the surge of life which is given at the moment of my conception and which will push my life forward throughout my existence. The original *qi* must be everywhere in order to make the *zang* function. This is the vital life-giving animation which is received when you receive life. And life will last as long as the original *qi* lasts. Here we can look at Nan jing difficulty 8. The question there is why, when the pulse seems to be completely in balance, do people die? The answer is that the original *qi* has been exhausted. When a tree dies by the roots then the leaves soon wither and die. *Zong qi* (宗 氣), the ancestral *qi*, is the way in which the *qi* finds its commanding power in a person, something which gathers it together under a single authority, and guarantees that all the *qi* is part of the same family and forms one single being.

Claude Larre: That is the foundation of immunology for the Chinese. *Zong qi* (宗 氣) accepts that which is proper and rejects that which is not compatible or similar.

Elisabeth Rochat: *Zong* (宗) has the sense of an ancestor, but not an ancestor as in the founder of a lineage or line. There is another character for that. It is more the sense of the lineage itself.

Claude Larre: The most simple example is to look at any chronology of Chinese dynasties with the name of the emperor. For example, the first in the Han dynasty is Gao Zu, but the others in the dynasty would be *zong*, (宗) with the *zong* of *zong qi*. This is because the others are the rightful successors in the lineage, they are the family tree.

Elisabeth Rochat: *Zong* (宗) also indicates he who is in charge of organizing and directing the cult of ancestors. He has the necessary authority for this because he is of the proper rank in the family, and he brings together all those who have the right to participate. So in *zong* there is this idea of gathering together for a higher function, and that is exactly what we saw with regard to the sea of *qi* in the centre of the chest in relation to the ancestral *qi* which brings together all *qi* under the same authority to direct its circulation and movement throughout the body. Life is perpetuated in an ancestral line in just the same way. It is the idea of gathering together in order to direct somewhere. You can also put the character *zong* with other characters, for example *mai* (脈) or *jin* (筋), and there is the same idea of bringing together in order to be able to direct the action.

Question: Does this lineage reflect the uniqueness of the person?

Claude Larre: The coherence of self is the same as the cohesion of the others. When somebody is agitated that person is unbearable for the neighbours and the family. The reason why we should be quiet is not just because it is good for us, it is good for others. There is nothing more unpleasant than being obliged to live in a family where somebody is not at rest. All life is shaken around. That is a question of *zong* (宗). If you are not able to be coherent then all others will suffer, but the more coherent you are yourself, the more the other people will naturally come together and arrange themselves in order around what you are doing, saying and living.

Elisabeth Rochat: *Zhen qi* (真 氣), authentic *qi*, is when everything that happens in my being conforms to what I should be. That is to say that the destiny which I received from heaven, called in Chinese *ming* (命), a mandate, which is nothing more than the best line I can make with what I have been given, is correctly followed. At this moment the quality of *qi* will conform to my nature, which is the same thing as conforming to my origin. This is called authenticity, and this is why we find this term *zhen* (真), authentic, as a synonym for original, *yuan* (元), and for the original *yin* and *yang* of the kidneys. An authentic man will be a man of very great saintliness. In Su wen chapter 1 the authentic men are at the highest level of saintliness, they are practically beyond heaven/earth.

Claude Larre: They are more saints than saintly men.

THE SPLEEN AND STOMACH

脾胃

pi wei zhe cang lin zhi guan
wu wei chu yan

脾胃者倉廩之官
五味出焉

The spleen and stomach are responsible
for the storehouses and granaries
The five tastes stem from them

Claude Larre: For the first time in the series there is now a combination of two *zang*. One is the spleen and the other is the stomach. There is something common in the two characters for spleen and stomach which is extraordinarily important to note. Both characters have the radical for flesh or part of the body (月), but in *pi* (脾) it is on the left side, and in *wei* (胃) it is underneath. It might have some meaning that the radical is not placed in the same position for both of them, but I will leave the interpretation of this to Elisabeth. *Guan* (官) we know is the function, or the charge. *Cang* (倉) and *lin* (廩) are two sorts of storage. One is storage to preserve, to collect and then to preserve what has been collected and to store what has been accepted from heaven. The other is a granary for distribution. So we have two characters which are very close to one another, with the sense of receiving in order to be able to distribute. Quite obviously what is produced by this collection and distribution is very important, and collection for distribution is what we call the five tastes or flavours, the *wei* (味).

Elisabeth Rochat: For the first time we find ourselves faced with a unique charge which is attributed to two viscera. But we must not be astonished by this because spleen and stomach continually work together. Spleen and stomach make up the middle heater, representing the junction of heaven and earth in man, and commanding the movements of raising and lowering. The spleen is the *zang* which is most directed towards the *fu* since it is through the spleen that everything drawn from food must pass before circulating in the body. As for the stomach, it has a particularly noble and elevated place because it is also a sea, the sea of liquids and cereals. In other words it is a sea for everything that is absolutely essential for the continuation of life. So the spleen and stomach form an ensemble which is indispensable, and which cannot be broken apart. The liver and gallbladder were intimately linked, but nevertheless they each had a particular charge, while the spleen and stomach together fulfil the same charge of being storehouse and granary. They receive and then store the grains or food, but if you put grain into a granary you do not just leave it there, it is stored so that it can be taken out when it is needed. For example, we store in the autumn so that we can live through the winter.

Claude Larre: It works both ways. What you need to sow in the field you take from the granary in spring, but what you harvest in the autumn you keep there during winter. As long as there is no production it is necessary to have reserves. This is true not only for grain but for any storage of life.

Elisabeth Rochat: If we want to differentiate between the two characters we can put *cang* (倉), the first character, on the side of the stomach for reception and storage. One name for stomach is *tai cang* (太 倉) meaning big storehouse. The spleen's function, on the other hand, is distribution and dispatching. The term often used with the spleen is *yun* (運), which is the distribution in all directions from the spleen of the essences and interstitial fluids and so on. This is more the granary, *lin* (廩), function. It is from the storehouses and granaries that everything which is needed to build up blood and *qi*, body fluids and flesh and so on, will come, and when the stomach receives correctly and the transformations are well made, and the essences necessary for life are extracted from the food, then the result of all this is what is called the five *wei* (味), the five tastes. The number five here is interesting because it represents the totality of life. It is the totality and the diversity of everything that will reconstitute life. In the character *wei* (味) we have the radical for mouth on the left (口) and an ear of corn on the right (未). When you say 'taste' you think of the taste that you might have in your mouth, but this taste is only the exterior manifestation of the interior or intimate nature of what one is eating at the time.

Just as colour is the exterior aspect of the intimate or essential nature of something, which is why heaven is seen as blue, earth as yellow and trees and vegetation as green, so taste is not just the impression that you have in the mouth. It is that which forms the basis of the impression that gives you the taste. It is the quality of the essences that constitute the food, and these essences are drawn out from the work done by the stomach and spleen. After extraction the essences go to the place with which they have an affinity. So if I eat something that has an acid, sour taste, it means that the materials that are full of life which constitute this food have some kind of relationship with the same movement that is found in the spring and wood. It is the same quality of *qi* that has created the liver and which has also made the muscular force, the tendons, in the body. So when I eat food it is completely broken down by the work of the middle heater in ripening and rotting, and a state of subtlety is arrived at which is called *jing wei* (精微). *Jing* (精) is the essences and *wei* (微) indicates something which is very fine and subtle, so refined that it has great power of penetration. It is the necessary route between what is not me and what is me. Everything that you eat will become your skin, your *qi* and everything else.

Claude Larre: Maybe I could add two remarks. One is that when you are refuelling your car in the petrol station you ask for high grade or low grade. The high grade is like the *jing wei* (精 微) and the low grade is like the *wu wei* (五 味), the five tastes. These are not the ultimate product, even though they may be alright. A representation of the best condition in which to be assimilated is not easily expressed by the five tastes, it is better to go further and say *jing wei* (精 微). Second, when you are refuelling your car if some part of the fuel spills out onto the car it will smell for quite a while. It is disseminated everywhere and it is not easily moved by the air. There is no end to the subtlety of exchanges, and no end to the taking into yourself of the environment. But you cannot take things in which are not prepared for you, and to receive properly you have to prepare yourself.

Elisabeth Rochat: Once this level of *jing wei* (精 微) is reached there is in these essences everything that is composed of the vitality of what I have eaten. Then there will again be a separation made in the *jing wei* and expressed in the form of the five tastes. So the acid, sour taste will invigorate the liver, and the same for the other four *zang*. You can see how diet can be very important, and constitutes a treatment in itself. There are very precise indications on this in the Su wen. So, the stomach receives all the food that is made up of the five tastes, and by the work of the stomach and spleen these same tastes will reconstitute my being.

THE LARGE INTESTINE

da chang zhe chuan dao zhi guan
bian hua chu yan

The large intestine is responsible for transit
The residue from transformation stems from it

Claude Larre: This is the large intestine, *da chang* (大腸). The other one is *xiao chang* (小腸), the small intestine. The function or charge is *chuan dao* (傳道). *Chuan* is to transmit, *dao* (道) means along the way or along the road, which we can call transit. So *chuan* (傳) is the progressive march of what is inside, but it is also the movement by which this transit is made.

Chuan (傳) has different meanings. One is not only to transmit but also in a way to specialize and make a distinction within the mass of what has been elaborated through the combination of *pi* (脾) and *wei* (胃). It is a continuation as well as an elaboration of the ingested material that has to be transmitted. During the process of transmission something more is done by the large intestine. But it is better to see the large and small intestines working together, and it is easier to explain one through the other rather than just taking one after the other.

Dao (道) is the same character as in Dao de jing, the Way and the Virtue. But here we understand it as the network by which what has been ingested and digested is now conducted through the organism to an end which will be partly assimilation and partly rejection. *Dao* (道) also has a meaning connected with the vital circulation, *mai* (脈), since they too are going in certain directions. It means the direction which, materially speaking, follows the current of nourishment. But immediately after the consideration of the location comes the consideration of the function. We have to see both at the same time, that there is a certain place where things are going, and there are certain activities of life which are accomplished in following that network. That is the meaning of *chuan dao* (傳 道), and *chuan dao* is the charge of the large intestine in comparison with the charge of the small intestine which is not said to work along a path, but which receives things, works on them and then disperses them throughout the organism.

Bian hua chu yan (變 化 出 焉) is a very important and subtle description of what the final product of the work done by the large intestine is. When I say product I am not referring to a material thing. It is important not to materialize what is said in the text. *Bian* (變) is a change, and *hua* (化) is another way to look at that change. Taken together, *bian hua* (變 化) is a fundamental expression in the field of Chinese medicine. Since we are now facing the problem of expression in two characters, normally we would think that *bian* is operated through heaven's power and *hua* is the answering of the formative activity of earth. When there is a *hua* there is a transformation actually made or in the making. When it is *bian* there is something in the process of change.

You are driving a car, and when you turn the wheel that is the change, but the fact that the vehicle is no longer in the same place and is now on another stretch of road, or another road entirely, that is *hua* (化). So with your wheel you are master of the direction and this is *bian* (變), and when your car is obediently going along another stretch of road that is *hua*. So *bian hua* (變化) as a typical expression in the vocabulary contains the heaven/earth operation which results in your benefit. It is the product or result of what is made by the large intestine, of the nourishment which has been ingested and digested, and at the same time the product or result of your own personal disposition. We are here in a situation of nourishment, and everything which has been said is said primarily about that nourishment, but at the same time it is also said of the person who benefits from the operation of being nourished.

THE SMALL INTESTINE

xiao chang zhe shou sheng zhi guan
hua wu chu yan

The small intestine is responsible
for receiving and making things thrive
Transformed substances stem from it

Claude Larre: Now we proceed to the small intestine. Small by opposition with large, and the contrast is an important fact. Of course large is large and small is small, but what is important is that the large is not the small and the small is not the large. Always keep in mind that the authors are not just writing one sentence after another. They say several things at the same time, and the concepts are together but the characters are disposed like any Occidental text, one after the other. That is why Elisabeth wants to take the large and small intestines and try to make comparisons and connections, and to use one to make the other better understood.

Elisabeth Rochat: Here there is an inversion in the presentation because the logical progression from the stomach would be the small intestine and not the large intestine. But the large always comes before the small, so when in Chinese you have *da* (大) and *xiao* (小), what is great or large cannot be put after what is small in the hierarchy. The large intestine is at the same time large in actual size, and also comes up above and around the small intestine. In chapter 8 we do not follow the actual pathway of the digestive tract, the different charges are given their natural hierarchical order.

Claude Larre: It might be that there are other reasons which we have not yet discovered for the order of presentation. Those reasons are good, but they are not very strong in themselves. Elisabeth has been looking through the main commentaries, but they do not speak very much on that subject. But it might be that if we are instituting parallels from one line to another we may find that there is some sort of design that we have not been able to discover up till now. It is also my feeling that immediately after the small intestine they have to talk about the triple heater and the bladder, so it is better that the small intestine is not too far away.

Comment: My feeling is that by studying the large intestine first you understand the process of all the intestines better because it sounds as if the small intestine is transitional between the stomach and the large intestine. The small intestine's function is more transitional, but you can see the whole process more clearly defined in the large intestine.

Claude Larre: It is true that the large intestine alludes to change, *bian hua* (變 化), and that maybe *bian hua* has to be talked about before *hua wu* (化 物). It is possible that *bian hua* is the direct change and that *hua wu* is the centre of that, externally speaking. That comes back to the explanation given by Elisabeth when she said that what is big has to be said before what is small, not only in terms of the hierarchy of pronouncements, but perhaps so that we first give the outline of the process, which is the large intestine at work, and then after that you restrict your consideration or focus to what is more essential for life. The large intestine transforms what has been ingested by the stomach, so it must come after the consideration of the spleen and stomach. It is the final part of the process initiated in the sixth line of the text when they talk of spleen and stomach. Spleen and stomach are at the entrance and the large intestine is at the exit, and what comes in the middle is based on that supposition. But, if it had been presented in the reverse order we would certainly find an equally clever reason why, so maybe we will just drop the issue!

Question: Is it also possible that the large intestine's function relates to the number seven and the small intestine to number eight?

Claude Larre: No, in fact that would be a reason for putting the small intestine first since the life power is more given by the small intestine than by the large intestine. That would be a reason for the reverse presentation.

What is the charge of the small intestine? The charge is *shou sheng* (受 盛). *Shou* (受) is to receive or to accept, with the understanding that something has been given, something has been transmitted, or something has been separated. So the small intestine is now ready to accept or receive the transformed material and use it to give to life the condition of prosperity and abundance which is characteristically expressed by the second character *sheng* (盛). *Sheng* (盛) is the character for the ascending process of life. When you say *shen qi sheng* (腎 氣 盛) you are saying that the *qi* from the kidneys is in the ascent. All the power and prosperity of life is seen, and all the development of life.

This is seen in Su wen chapter 1 where the little girl of seven is said to be in a state where the kidneys are in full swing. Then the man at sixteen is in a condition in which he has got tremendous power coming from the kidneys, and this continues for some time before it starts to decline. The same is true for the history of a dynasty. There is at first, a period of foundation, followed by organization, and then everything is renewed again and the old dynasty is destroyed. There comes a time when all the forces of the nation are mobilized through the leadership of a man who has received the mandate of heaven, and he gives a good start to the dynasty. His successors are able to maintain this organized power, making the country properous and giving happiness to the citizens. But the time will come when there is no more incentive to work, and then there is a decline. We can see that in an individual life, in the life of any organization or in the life of an empire - there is always an opening, always a foundation, and then the prosperity grows, up to a certain point. But it must necessarily decline, even if it seems accidental. And the Chinese are very sensitive to the effect of the ascending and descending, and the reascending, through the flux of life. But the meaning here in *shou sheng* (受 盛) is that first we have to receive, accept, take in, and then the effect of that is that life is stronger.

The product of the small intestines is that the food has become part of your own body. That state of affairs is called *hua wu* (化物). The things which you have digested are no longer in the state they once were, they are yourself. They are transformed substances. Things are now perfectly transformed, and totally assimilated into yourself. There is a connection between the two *hua* (化), the *bian hua* (變化) and the *hua wu* (化 物) which may be the turning point for understanding the presentation of the large and small intestines.

Elisabeth Rochat: The *fu* which are in charge of digestion (*chuan hua zhi fu* 傳 化 之 腑), are for transmission and transformation. This is summed up in the character which we saw with the large intestine, *chuan* (傳). This group is formed by the stomach, the two intestines, the triple heater and the bladder. It is therefore normal that we would find this character *hua* (化) repeated here. We did not find it with the stomach because the stomach is enhanced by its relation with the spleen, and because in the Nei jing the stomach is generally considered as the place from which all nutrition for the being comes. It is for that reason that what result from its charge are the five tastes. But when we come to the intestines we enter the realm of tranformation and transmission of matter. This is not to say that there has not been transformation and transportation before at the level of the stomach and spleen, because the charge of the spleen is also to ensure transformation and transmission, but it is not the same character as used for the large intestine, *chuan* (傳), it is a different one for dispatching and distributing.

Claude Larre: One more word here. There are people who are in charge of making other people work, and that is the case with the spleen. It is then difficult to call that transformation.

It is giving orders that are very carefully worded and directed to people, distributing work, assigning things to everybody and making sure the materials and tools are ready. That is not transmission and transportation.

Elisabeth Rochat: At the level of the small intestine there is also an extremely important operation which takes place, and that is called the separation of the clear and the unclear. At the level of the stomach the first extraction of what is essential is made, and at the level of the small intestine, in the depths of the body, there is a separation that takes place in the transformed food. This operation of separation and tranformation is in two directions. In the separation of clear and unclear there is the extraction of the juices and liquids which are useful to life, and which pass into the general circulation of liquids. Then there is the continued descent through the body of what is not useable by the small intestine. What is heavier, more condensed, more materialized and solid will be transported towards the large intestine, and what is more liquid, lighter and of finer texture will be transported to the bladder. So the small intestine operates on and makes the best use of everything that comes to it from the stomach. But at that point there is a definite separation.

Claude Larre: The vitality comes from that operation and gives this character *sheng* (盛). Everything is carried to the utmost, to maximize the vitality.

Elisabeth Rochat: But the small intestine does not operate the final changes which ensure that from these vital substances inside the body I can draw what is essential and vital for me, and that when nothing further can be taken from them that they become matter which will leave my body. For the small intestine the results of the function of transformation will go on towards the bladder and the large intestine. This is the logical sequence of operations. Life is just a perpetual transformation. In the large intestine there is not only the work of drying and extraction of substances, there are also changes and transformation. There is the change whereby that which could potentially bring me vitality becomes something which no longer holds anything of value for me.

We saw earlier the character *jing* (精) which represents the essences, and which is composed of a kind of bursting seed on the left, and the green colour manifesting life, corresponding to the east and spring on the right. In the character *po* (粕) which represents the residues or wastes, you have the same seed or grain on the left, but instead of adding the green of rising life we have the image of white (白), corresponding to the west, the autumn and the decline of life. *Po* (粕) represents the point where nothing more can be extracted to help or form life. It also has the same sound and phonetic as the *po* (魄) which is associated with the lungs. These *po* have the same descending and lowering movement as the residue. In Chinese the anus is called the gate or door of the *po*.

Claude Larre: *Po* with the two meanings.

Elisabeth Rochat: Yes, the *po* can be written with either character depending on whether you are looking at it from the point of view of digestion or on the level of your entire life. At the end of your life the *hun* (魂) rise up to heaven and the *po* which can no longer sustain life, descend and leave your being.

Claude Larre: This is very clearly seen with street cleaners and garbage. Garbage is the material we have to dispose of, but somebody has to take care of it, and those people are the street cleaners. When the *po*, residue, has disappeared then the people in charge of it have to disappear as well, and if they do not they become errant souls. This is a real problem for the Chinese. They make sure that the parts which no longer pertain to the spiritual source are correctly disposed of, and this is the reason why they take so much care in the burial rites of the left-over of a living person.

Comment: Traditionally they would also have jade plugs, one of which would go in the anus to stop up the *po*.

Claude Larre: Yes, when they put those jade stones on the mouth and all the openings it was just in order to block the *po* inside. The *po* then gradually lose their power and become extinct, because their vitality is connected with the remains of the deceased person. This is very logical, and you cannot separate the burial ritual from the Nei jing because it is all one civilization. It is enough for Occidental medicine to say that all excretion has been evacuated from the anus, but that is not enough for the Chinese. They ask what happens to the *po* (魄), the souls which are linked with this garbage and disposal of remains and residues?

Question: How do the *po* fit in with the lungs?

Elisabeth Rochat: The link is in the breathing, the natural rhythm of life, which is done by the branching, vegetation-like structure of the lungs that we saw in the character *fei* (肺) earlier. This is the relationship with vegetative life, and the *po* are on the side of vegetative life.

Claude Larre: Yes, this is the so-called animal life in a man, there is no resonance with the higher part.

Elisabeth Rochat: There is perhaps something more complex. A bird needs a branch to rest on! There is always the need for a crossing in any couple, the *qi* and the blood need to cross, *yin* and *yang* need to cross in order to be useful. The liver has this double aspect of emanating an enormous quantity of *qi* which is of great strength, but its foundation and basic substance is on the side of *yin*, the blood. The liver stores the blood and because of the *qi* of the liver it is correctly stored as well and does not just go everywhere in the body. For the same reason the *hun* (魂), which are on the side of the *qi*, need the liver to be full of blood in order to stay in their residence. It is the same principle as a bird needing to attach itself and perch on a branch.

You can see the pathology in a very simple example. When you have a case of emptiness of the blood in the liver, then very often the person affected has many strong and vivid dreams, and this is explained by saying that the *hun* are no longer housed in their residence. So you see that when the liver has insufficient blood to serve as a support for the *hun* then these *hun*, which are of the same nature as *qi* and therefore airy, can escape and this provokes disordered dreams.

By contrast the lungs are in contact with exterior air through respiration, and they are the master of *qi* for the whole body. It is from the upper heater that the *qi* comes out in rhythmic movement. The lungs are therefore the ideal residence for the *po* which are on the side of the essences. The *hun* are on the side of the *qi* and the *po* are on the side of the *jing* (精). This is a very traditional distinction in non-medical texts as well. After death the *hun* rise up to heaven where they become the manes, the spirits of the ancestors, and the *po*, who are on the side of vegetative animation and *jing* and of what maintains all the forms that come from the earth, return to the earth, where they slowly dissolve and disappear. What they are composed of will reconcile with the other elements there.

So some kind of crossing takes place because the liver has everything that is needed in its *yin* nature to retain the *hun* and the lung has everything in its expansive, breathlike nature to retain the *po*. If it was the other way round and the *po* were linked to the liver there would be inundation or stagnation, and if the *hun* were linked to the lungs there would be continual confusion and fireworks. That is what makes life, that the *hun* and *po* can be joined together like that. And when they are apart, it is death.

Claude Larre: We know that the anus is a door, *men* (門), an exit. And if there is an exit at this part of the body it is an exit at the end of a process. What is in location the lower part, is in function the final state. At the exit the *po*, the vegetative souls, go out, and at the same time the materials which are of no more use for the body are disposed of as garbage. When a person dies there is exactly the same process as for the garbage. The *po* and the garbage are taken back by earth, and go down to the Yellow Sources where all no longer usable material is in store waiting to come back to life in another form. It is a recycling process. Between the beginning at the stomach and spleen, where food is worked on to give it a condition in which it is nearly usable by the body, and the end at the large intestine, life is fertilized or nourished by a process of extraction performed by the large and small intestines.

This process is seen in the beginning with *hua* (化) and at the end which is *wu* (物). *Hua* is the transformation which is so perfect that finally life in myself comes to a position of being well-sustained or even enhanced and placed on a higher level. The materials are usable because they have been transformed. But the final transformation looks to the no longer usable. From this we may understand why they talk of the large intestine first and of the small intestine second. They give the whole process in its entirety from transformation to the final stage. This is transformation for life and transformation for disposal.

Everything that has been said about the clear and unclear has to do here with the distinction between *hua* (化) and *wu.*(物). Some things are sent down and some are sent up. We saw before that the vegetative life is under the administration of the lungs, and that there is a connection between the *po* (魄) as spirits and the *po* (粕) as residue because of the same phonetic, the colour white. We now understand that the residue is very close to the *po*, spirits, and that is the reason why they both go out of the body through the same door, and are both under the authority of the lungs.

THE KIDNEYS

shen zhe zuo qiang zhi guan
ji qiao chu yan

*The kidneys are responsible for the arousing of power
Skill and ability stem from them*

Claude Larre: Now we come to the kidneys. I will leave the explanation of why they appear so late in the text to Elisabeth. *Shen zhe* (腎者) is the kidneys, *zuo* (作) is a bursting activity and *qiang* (強) is fortitude. We come here to the natural, positive state of the kidneys which is to have control of life in ourselves, seen in the very fact that life is active. The charge or the responsibility for life of the kidneys is seen in the making, *zuo* (作), but the expansion of the *zuo* is the fortitude and strength. An activity tending to build strength in the flux of life is not a development of the body as such, it is a developing of strength itself, and such development of the body is not only related to bones and flesh and joints and so on.

Of course, everything being related to everything else, you may say that the kidneys are responsible for the solidity of the body, and in Su wen chapter 1 the force which is constantly alluded to is the *qi* of the kidneys. In chapter 1 if you look at the way in which a woman and a man develop, you have to go through the stages of development of their kidney *qi*. At a certain point you see that the body is very strong. But this is only one stage, and to understand the fullness of the role of the kidneys you have to take every stage into account. The fact that the young girl has beautiful hair and white, bright teeth is because there is a surplus in the activity of the kidneys in the body, and this has something to do with *zuo*. In common language *zuo* means to do or to make, but this is the weakest meaning.

Close to the root of the character is the sense that something narrow is being pressed between the sides of a container and wants to surge forth. The left part of the character is the radical for man, being a symbol of activity. It has something to do with sexual activity since we know that the centre of power or activity is related to the sexual constitution of man and woman.

The character *qiang* (強) contains the double bow, with all the implications of something strong and robust, and the preparation for springing out or shooting. The motion itself is always more important than the idea we might have about the motion! The result, the effect or the product of the kidneys is *ji qiao* (技 巧). *Ji* (技) has something to do with techniques, arts and craftsmanship. This is seen in the radical of the hand. It is the way to do things with the hands. *Ji shu* (技 術) is the ordinary expression for all the arts. *Qiao* (巧) has the meaning of very clever activity. *Ji* (技) is just know-how, but *qiao* (巧) is perfect know-how, with skill and rapidity, perfection and ease. *Qiao* is a quality of the brain, like the mind turning rapidly and without effort. So there is a connection between the kidneys and this burst of activity which tends towards fortitude and strength.

Elisabeth Rochat: We can take two examples to see how the kidneys are this contained force or strength, which is both the basis of the body and also maintains it. We can express this differently by saying that the kidneys store the essences because the essences are the basis of vitality, not only for the exhalation of *qi*, but also for the strength, uprightness, and the correctness of life. For example, in stimulating the power of the essences, the kidneys will build up their marrow, and when the marrow is well constituted then the bones will form and be full of strength. There is an excitation, a movement and an activity which is at the level of the marrow, and then a strength which is at the level of the bones. Commentaries like this are traditionally made in China to show how the kidneys, which always have a double aspect, construct the inner power of the being which will ensure its solidity.

The other example is that the kidneys store the essences while the heart is the dwelling place of the *shen* (神). The expression essences/spirits, *jing shen* (精 神), is therefore the expression that denotes life and vitality at its highest level, the vital spirit.

Claude Larre: When you go to a concert, if the conductor is full of *jing shen* then everybody playing instruments and in the audience will be seized by a common spirit and elation in their minds. Everything will rise up. Why? Because the essences have been activated by the conductor, and the feeling you have is nearly physical. You feel the music with all your body, mind and spirit. That is an example of *jing shen*. Or if you go to an art gallery and see a lot of Chagal or Turner paintings, you think, how is it possible that a man could be so clever and so inspired that everything is touched in the same manner and gives such an extraordinary impression of the forces of the universe? Then you can say that this painter is a man of *jing shen*. It is so well organized that it flows and flourishes.

Elisabeth Rochat: The essences which are fundamentally dependent on the kidneys serve as the support and basis for the spirits. This connection between the kidneys and the heart, given by *shao yin* (少 陰), establishes the central axis for vitality. So if on one hand the marrow and the bones are solid, and on the other the spirits can seize and rely on essences that are of good quality, then you will be able to live with all the know-how, skill and ability that is necessary for life. This is 'savoir vivre' in the sense of knowing how to live. It is because the marrow and the bones are there that you can make movements and can stand upright, and know how to direct your awareness through the clarity of the spirits.

Claude Larre: This is being able to conduct one's own life at the highest level of operation, with strong will, strong purpose, clear ideas and good feelings. All this is under the charge of the kidneys. It is a question of conducting, and you conduct life from the bottom to the top. The conducting relies on the bones and marrow and the essences which are stored in the kidneys.

Elisabeth Rochat: Now we come to the question of why the kidneys come in the ninth position in this presentation. We can say that nine, which is three times three, is a number of power.

Claude Larre: We saw that previously in the Temple of Heaven. And by the way, the heart meridian has nine points and the kidney meridian has 27, three times nine. This is significant.

Elisabeth Rochat: The kidneys come in this position, as if they were in an inferior position, because they represent life in the depths, in the invisible beginnings and in the seed. From this basis the fire of life will emerge, the fire which comes out of the water and which is expressed by the *shao yang* (少 陽), and by the fire of the heart which is the supreme development of this fire of life. At that moment the kidneys are no more than the permanent and original basis for life. That is to say, the fire of the kidneys, the fire of *ming men* (命 門), is continually active right up until the death of an individual. So Su wen chapter 8 is taking account of the concentrated power of the kidneys as the basis of life, like the foundations of a house. I think this is the reason that they are presented in this position in the text. It is not that they are less noble than the intestines, it is just that in the presentation of the whole ensemble they are in the depths.

Claude Larre: You may ask why we have chosen to explain it in this way. It is because their product or effect is given at the highest level. If the text just said that the kidneys are for the domestic chores of life, then it would be impossible to say that they are the basis of all life, but since they say that the final product is *ji qiao* (技 巧), we have to see that this activity which is embodied with some genius for life is something very noble.

In fact it is very clever of the man who made this presentation of the *zang* to dare not to follow the ordinary order.

Elisabeth Rochat: We must not forget what has been said about the kidneys in relation to sex and reproduction. The substance which is most charged with life and essences is the sperm. In Chinese this is called *jing* (精), which is exactly the same character as for essences. It has to be translated depending on the context. So in the kidneys there is not only the savoir vivre, the know-how and ability, but also the knowledge of how to create another life. It is this skill and ability which is shared between man and woman so that a new life can appear. The sexual aspect turned towards procreation is found in the expression *zuo qiang* (作 強), and the strongest, most manifest expression of the arousing of power is the life that you have created with your own life.

Claude Larre: There is a clue to this in Lao zi chapter 16 where it says: the ten thousand beings, being altogether, burst into life, and I myself am just there to contemplate their return. They burst into life, but all of them come back to their roots.

Question: What is their return?

Claude Larre: Their return is that recycling of life. Therefore I am not surprised to see that life is coming forth from every corner, but I am sage enough to see that the true law of this bursting is that it has to come back to its own roots, even for living. It is not that I am contemplating death in life, it is that I am seeing the proper movement of life that is inscribed in every progression of life and which is to come back to its roots. I see how the *hun* (魂) expand everywhere, but I understand that they have to be contained and more or less detained by the *po* (魄) in order that they not go too far and escape my control. If they escape my control they destroy me. So this *zuo* (作) character is really something to do with sexual activity in the large, broad meaning that life is given by it.

Coming back to the small intestine, we have been talking about transformed things and matter, but the most transformed of all things are actually the essences which are in the kidneys. So there is a link between this line of the large intestine and this line of the kidneys. We have to renew the essences up to the point where we renew their fertility. If they are fertile enough for reproduction, they are fertile for activity, and they are fertile enough to also give more sense to my own branch of life. It is the same thing. Activity, solidity, power for reproduction, they are all the same. That is the most essential part of the essences.

Elisabeth Rochat: This rising of the essences is made in a very subtle, fine manner to serve as a support for the spirits of the heart. This is the opposite of the more material way in which the essences surge out from below when they are represented as sperm. This very fine and subtle movement of essences is carried up towards the head, the round image of heaven at the highest point in an individual, where only what is most clear and pure can reach. Within the bones of the head is the brain, and the brain has one aspect which is *yin*, the marrow, and one aspect which is *yang*, the penetration of the spirits. The brain is equally called the *fu* (府) of the original spirits.

So we can see that this rising of life finds its centre in the heart and its expansion in the head, not only with the brain but with all the orifices which allow penetration and communication, and which are the superior orifices for what is clear and in the realm of *qi* and spirits. The mouth occupies a position which is in the middle between the ears, eyes and nose, through which the more refined and subtle things - hearing, vision and smell - pass, and the lower orifices which have a connection with the mouth and through which pass substances which are visible and materialised, either empty of life in the form of waste products, or charged with life in the form of sperm.

But the most important functions for the life of man are in the head, referring to everything that is most heavenly. For example, the meridian of the heart has a pathway which passes from the system of connections of the heart, *xin xi* (心 系), and goes up to the interior workings of the eye. Therefore there is a connection between the heart and the brain and with everything that takes place when you have vision. Of course, this does not prevent the eye from also being linked with the liver. Another example is that the kidneys have an intimate connection with the ear.

Question: Why is the kidney connected with the ear?

Elisabeth Rochat: There is the question of shape or form, where shape is indicative of the deep nature of something. If the ear, like the kidneys, has the shape of a crescent moon, it indicates that there is a deep connection between the two. This is a connection between the depths of life and the reception of life, because just as the moon receives the light of the sun, so the ears receive all the time. So the kidneys are that which continually receives and stores the essences of life.

THE TRIPLE HEATER

三焦

san jiao zhe jue du zhi guan
shui dao chu yan 水

三焦者決瀆之官
水道出焉

The triple heater is responsible for the opening up of passages and irrigation
The regulation of waterways stems from it

Claude Larre: The triple heater is in charge of something which is called *jue du* (決 瀆). Both characters contain the water radical, but they do not have the same meaning. *Jue* (決) is always the first character and *du* (瀆) is an extension or a complementary aspect of *jue*. *Jue* (決) is to make a determination of how things flow. Historically Emperor Yu, the founder of the first Xia dynasty, was able to control the flow of rivers in China and thereby changed the destiny of the country. *Jue* (決) was found previously in relation to the gallbladder, so it has a connection with the *shao yang* (少 陽) and the creating of circulation and deciding what passage to take. *Du* (瀆) means a ditch, a drain or a canal. It is also used to describe one of the four great rivers of China.

So it is interesting to see that though we talk of heat or fire, or the triple heater, the function has more to do with the channelling and the circulation of liquids. But the final product, *shui dao* (水 道), seems to have nothing to do with fire. *Shui dao* (水 道) means the direction of all the rivers and waterways in the organism, just as might be seen in the empire. We have to understand something which not seen so much in Europe where the rivers are not as important, because the control of water has been and still is one of the main preoccupations of the Chinese. This vocabulary comes from ancient history and reveals that the way the Chinese understood life in an individual was the same as the way they understood the control of life in the empire.

But the question of water does have something to do with the question of fire. Life is like a sort of cooking where you cannot really use fire without water and you cannot really use water without fire. You have to be at a certain degrees of temperature in order to get all the essences. This is controlled between fire and water.

Elisabeth Rochat: It should be noticed that for the first time since the heart we have a viscera which does not have the flesh or part of the body radical (月) in the character. This is because the triple heater has no form. It just has some points of command and some functions. It has expression but no actual place where you can say that its function is located. You can simply say that it is triple, it is a three, and three means that we enter the world of *qi* moving in the median void. The triple heater will always have something to do with *qi* and with mediation, being a go-between. We have already seen how it was the messenger of the original *qi* and the representative of the fire of *ming men* (命 門) which allows all life to continue.

The four strokes that you see beneath the character *jiao* (焦) represent fire, just like the fire beneath the cooking pot. In chapter 8 of the Su wen we cannot speak of the triple heater as encircling or encompassing all the other functions, we are rather forced to allocate it a particular function.

Claude Larre: Why?

Elisabeth Rochat: In order to correlate it with the other functions at the same level, it has to be described in its most concrete sense, in charge of the drainage of liquids of the body. But this function has repercussions on the whole body. In terms of other *zang* connected with the liquids of the body we have the kidneys which are responsible for water in the lower heater, the spleen being responsible for the production and diffusion of the *jin ye* (津液), body fluids, in the middle heater, and the lungs responsible for the regulation of liquids in the upper heater. It is all this ensemble of the circulation which we put together and which becomes the unity of the triple heater.

There is, in the Nei jing, important pathology particularly linked to swellings and oedema on the body which is linked to the triple heater in its function of being in charge of the correct conduct and regulation of liquids. It is obvious that the conduction of liquids cannot be made except under the government of the *qi*, and it is also obvious that the liquids which arrive in the lower part of the body are transformed by the kidneys and bladder. One part will be rejected from the body and the other will be reused after purification. At that moment it will be clear and therefore useful to life. Under the action of the fire of *ming men* (命門) it will be able to evaporate and rise up in a vapour throughout the whole body. Afterwards there comes the descending function of the lungs and so on, and the reconstitution that derives from the stomach and spleen.

THE BLADDER

膀胱

pang guang zhe zhou du zhi guan
jin ye cang yan
qi hua ze neng chu yi

膀胱者州都之官
津液藏焉
氣化則能出矣

The bladder is responsible for regions and cities
It stores the body fluids
The transformations of the qi then give out their power

Claude Larre: The bladder is very similar to what we saw for the triple heater, but it does not speak so much of water. It has the longest description, and the structure of the text is not the same as the others. There is something final in this statement. That is why there are more characters.

The charge has something to do with what is called *zhou* (州) in Chinese. When water is clearly separated from the ground, or when in a river there are small, neatly separated islets, then the population may live from tilling the fields and they have the means of travel from one city to another on boats. The implication is that in the empire or in our own bodies it is very important to be sure that water stays in its place and is clearly separated from firm ground. This is the idea of *zhou*. *Du* (都) is a capital, in the way that Beijing is the northern capital and Nanjing is the southern capital. *Du* (都) with the character *zhou* (州) means to have a good establishment for the capital, the administration, the emperor, the court, the palace and so on, on a firm piece of land. So we understand that the bladder must have charge of some sort of territorial organization where the water and the earth are well separated, and it can control and keep the established situation in good state.

The outcome or product of the bladder is something we would not have guessed from the charge. It is that the *qi*, being transformed, is then able to appear. But between the function and this product there is an intermediary statement which is *jin ye cang yan* (津 液 藏 焉). The translation of the whole line would be: the charge of the bladder is to constitute territories where water and firm ground will be clearly and distinctly separated, that something is established for government administration, and then through the storing and preservation of the *jin ye* (津 液) it is possible for *qi* to appear after its transformation. It does not say that *qi* appears, it says that it is possible for it to appear. Or, if you interpret it slightly differently, it says that then it is able and strong enough to appear, and the better the bladder does its work, the richer the transformed *qi* is, and in association with blood is capable of assuming all the duties of a living person. To appear is to appear to work.

When it says *qi hua* (氣 化) it means all the transformations which are proper to the *qi*, which is itself proper to myself after the transformations. Before transformation the *qi* in any food might be transformed differently according to a person's individual, specific and different *zang* . So here, at the end of the process we come to see that the bladder has the role of making clear distinctions in this immense territory of the body in order for it to achieve life. This is exactly how a safe ruler, after having made a good separation of water and land, is able to have people working and enjoying life through the production of *qi* coming from this division. So there is a connection between the charge and the product, and the kind of water it is. Then if we refer to the final stage where life is appearing through the transformation of *qi*, then the intermediaries are the *jin ye* (津液). If anyone asks whether the study of *jin ye* is important, the answer is that at the end of this chapter they are shown in an exceptionally bright light, since the construction is made so that we can see the importance given to them.

Elisabeth Rochat: It is astonishing that the only time we meet the character *cang* (藏) in this passage which is concerned with the twelve *zang* is right at the end and in relation to the bladder, which some people in the west consider a very secondary organ. The bladder is not only seen with its function of elimination, you could even say that that hardly appears in this text. It comes at the end, but there is still something that proceeds from it. *Qi hua* (氣 化) can be understood as the residue of the transformation, but it is much more commonly used to mean the way in which the whole universe lives and is animated. Everything that lives in the world is concerned with the transformation of *qi*, both how the *qi* is transformed and how the *qi* makes the transformations. The whole process of life is that from the essences come the *qi* that itself sets off all the functioning of life. And because of this work of transformation it will produce beings that are made of essences. It is a kind of cycle of life in the universe.

Claude Larre: The problem is that usually, when you talk of a subject you are limited to that subject, but since the analogy of the process is already in the mind of the Chinese, when we make a statement it is just to open up the field. Then we are obliged to call to our rescue all the other elements which cooperate to make universal life. When they talk of how the *qi* is produced in me they do not only talk of how I produce *qi* myself, they extend it to the universe, and the generation of life which comes from me is understood, as are the ancestors who gave me all my genetic makeup.

Elisabeth Rochat: Life in a human being is the same as the life of the universe. I take essences, I possess them, and from them continually emanates the *qi* that makes all the subtle mechanisms of life work in myself, especially allowing the *zang* to store this life in the form of essences as a provision for the future emanation of *qi*. That is the function of the *zang*.

Claude Larre: In French we use 'thesaurisation' for *zang*. 'Thesauriser' means to keep very closely and sometimes to add something. It is like when you have plants in a greenhouse and they are actively treated and preserved, that process is typical of what happens in a *zang*.

Comment: 'Distil' is quite good because you put in hops and it ferments to make beer. They are stored but they are also developing. Or 'to treasure'?

Claude Larre: 'To treasure' has two meanings in English. To like very much and to keep very, very preciously. The word *zang* is much better. If there is no word that we are able to devise, then just turn to the Chinese word!

Elisabeth Rochat: The transformation of *qi*, *qi hua* (氣 化), is a way of indicating all the phenomena of life in an individual. A particular use of this expression is when you use it to refer to the lower heater, to the particular region of bladder and kidneys. That is to say, the transformation of *qi* which is produced by the activity of *ming men* (命 門). It is because of this that the text of Su wen chapter 8 says that the transformation of *qi* has the potential of giving out that power. This transformation of *qi* is also there to sum up and encompass all the twelve charges we have previously mentioned, because these charges are nothing other than the transformation of *qi* and the becoming of the essences in the light of the spirits.

So it is with the bladder, being the *tai yang* (太 陽) turned towards the exterior of the body, that you find the term *cang* (藏), to store, to preserve and conserve on the interior. This *cang* is made for all the liquids in the body, and it is used in contrast to the concept of flowing and evacuating. To show the regulation that the bladder has on the body's liquids it is important to see it in the liquids that it puts back into the circulation of the body and those it eliminates. In a restricted sense the *qi hua* (氣 化) is the work done on the liquids which arrive in the lower part of the body for purification or throwing out. That part which is clarified and still charged with life is put back into circulation by the action of the kidneys, the fire of *ming men* (命 門) and all the workings of the triple heater.

This charge of the bladder is very difficult to grasp, and since it comes last there is both the specificity of its function and a recapitulation of everything which has gone before. That which has a position below and which commands by being below, has a way of directing and controlling the whole ensemble. It brings together all the functions which are found elsewhere. This is completely different from the control of the heart. It is important to underline that the bladder, which seems so unimportant, has in reality an action of control which is very great. It controls, by eliminating or re-injecting into the body, the quantity and quality of liquids from below. It determines the quantity of liquids which will irrigate all the parts of the body, all the flesh and the muscular power which runs through the flesh. The *tai yang* (太 陽) meridian of the foot has a particular action on the muscles, and by virtue of its pathway up the back, governs all the attachments of the muscles of the back. The meridian which is the expression of the bladder allows us to understand the extension of the power of the bladder a little better.

And we always come back to the kidneys with their double storing of fire and water. There are two *fu* (府) that are linked to the kidneys in the Nei jing. There is the triple heater which takes charge of the fire of *ming men* (命 門), and on the other hand there is the bladder which takes account of the water side of the kidneys. From the waters of the bladder come the regulation that is called *tai yang* (太 陽), which is the greatest expansion of *yang* and the principle heir of *du mai* (督 脈).

The bladder controls the quantity and quality of the liquids, while the triple heater controls their regulation and movement.

So it is through the ensemble of the lower heater and of the sea of *qi* below that the transformation is made, especially through all this work on the liquids. In a more general fashion it is in this way that all the *qi hua* (氣 化) are accomplished to make the life of the being through the twelve charges or the twelve *zang*. This is the power of life, the potential of being able to live.

CONCLUSION

*Fan ci shi er guan zhe
bu de xiang shi ye*

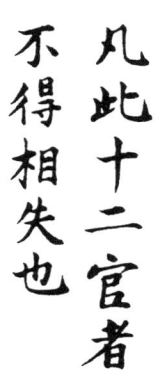

凡此十二官者
不得相失也

*These twelve charges form an interdependent
group that allows of no failing*

Claude Larre: They cannot really do anything other than cooperate. The beginning of the text alluded to the same thing when it said they help one another. So at the end it says they cannot not help one another. The *xiang* (相), mutual action, is the same character as appeared in the first line of the chapter. There the emperor's question was which one is noble and which one is less noble? Now the question is more what does it mean to be noble or less noble? To be noble or not does not make any difference to the efficiency. It is important in society that noble and less noble work in such a manner that the noble never presses on the less noble, and that the less noble never disobey the noble. Why it is so? Just because it is nature!

If in nature heaven is not earth and if man is made at the crossing of the heaven/earth power, then it is necessary in any situation, be it empire, court, administration, or an individual life, to recognize things as they are and to understand that we have to start with the head of the power, which is this silent place of the heart. All the others come one after another to complete the picture of a total life. Sometimes they are very close to each other like the liver and gallbladder or the spleen and stomach, and the explanation can be given in a united and concise way.

I am sure that the kidneys, triple heater and bladder might also be seen as an ensemble. But if you take the heart or the bladder together you see that they are in perfect control of the whole situation, though not from the same point of view. If you take the triple heater and bladder you have some sort of universal functioning for the last stages of the operation of life. Besides, if the description of all the charges goes in an orderly way, there is a recapitulation of what has been said before, and sometimes it is more visible or more important. That might be why the bladder has this longer expression and gives the impression that the liquids, being in the middle, are some sort of mediation between the innermost part of ourselves and the atmospheric environment in which all our life is contained.

So chapter 8 is very, very short. We have explained only a few characters, but this is the way to explore the Chinese language as the repository of knowledge. We have maps, a map of the five elements or a map of this and that, but the most useful map is not one with European words. The most useful map is one with a few Chinese characters well connected one with another. The Chinese text holds the essence of the seminar. We must work with a free circulation of expression and in all languages, and that will be the liquid, the *jin ye* (津 液), that we need for the circulation of life.

The text continues:

If then the sovereign radiates (virtue) those under him will be at peace. From this the nurturing of life will give longevity, from generation to generation, and the empire will radiate with a great light.

But if the sovereign does not radiate (virtue), the twelve charges will be in danger which will cause the closing and blocking of the ways, finally stopping communication and the body will be seriously injured. From this the nurturing of life will sink into disaster. Everything that lives under heaven will be threatened in its ancestral line with the greatest of dangers.

Take care, I repeat, take good care!

Claude Larre: There is nothing to add, it is so simple. One may say that this final conclusion comes like a warning, particularly to the people in charge. The first one in charge is the *jun zhu* (君 主). We saw that the emperor, being an emperor, is the master either directly or through the prime minister. In myself it is through the heart that I am sovereign and master of myself. There is no difference between myself and my heart as far as sovereignty and government are concerned. *Ming* (明) is a character made by the association of sun and moon. It implies all the light coming from the sun in daylight and the moon at night. There is also the distinction between the light which is radiant by itself and the light which is communicated by the sun to the moon. The combination of the two implies the distinction between the two components. The full richness of the meaning of things is in the completion of components and at the same time the distinction between the two parts or many other parts that join together.

If the sovereign or the heart is really radiating its virtue, which is communicated by heaven, then the people will feel the communication between themselves and the emperor through all the agents and officials. The feeling in the people is that since the emperor is really observing the mandate of heaven, it is certain that heaven will show benevolence and will pour favours onto the emperor and the imperial administration, and that will enrich all the citizens of the empire. The crops will be good, there will be no earthquakes or floods. This was the creed of Chinese society, and it is very interesting for us since we understand that spiritual life is a part of life just as food and drink are part of life.

There is no point in people who are not in control of themselves going to an acupuncturist except to receive a lesson on how to live. Psychological or psychoanalytic treatment is normal for an acupuncturist since he cannot really separate the origin of the trouble. We are prepared to restore peace in the person and we do that according to this pronouncement which is that if it is good for the empire it is equally good for any individual. It is the same thing. We have to get used to it, that a person and society are just one thing as far as the communication of life is given. As for the law and the organization of society with official duties and so on, that is different, it is organization by law. But above the law there is the law of nature which is about things as they are, and it is proper to the living being to be incorporated into this bigger group.

So if the sovereign is not really true to his mandate the twelve charges will be in danger. To be in danger, *wei* (危), is a typical Chinese expression. The character shows a man who ventures onto a rocky hill and does not know how to get down. This is a dangerous situation.

Elisabeth Rochat: You find this character *wei* (危) in the character for the gallbladder (膽).

Claude Larre: There is a reason for that. The gallbladder is some sort of equilibrium for life, and life being in some sort of harmony, in order to live has to come into some sort of disharmony. It is exactly the same thing as walking. You stretch your leg and incline your body to take the first step, but if you do it too much you fall down. Then you have to move the other leg in front of the first one, and the equilibrium is restored. This principle is that life is a disequilibrium, up to a certain point, which has to be brought back into harmony. So the twelve charges would be in danger if the principle of all the administration ruling the body was not working. They would give the explanation that what is necessary for life is free communication, *tong* (通). If communication is no longer free, first there is a closing, and then if that is definite there is an obstruction, and then there is no more communication and the body will suffer from internal disorder.

Elisabeth Rochat: This character *tong* (通) is very important. There is a strength behind it. It is free circulation and inter-communication which is well-made and well-maintained. There are two parts to the character. The left and underneath part is the radical for walking, marching, going and circulating. The central part has a double idea. It is at once something surging and springing up, and also something that is useful, which gives service and gives all its capacity. When you have the two parts together you have the idea of something there in order to give service, which is full of the power of springing up and which is animated by a circulation or a movement which nothing can stop. It is a character used at all levels. On the highest it is the communication that each being has with heaven, and it is this that maintains it in life. Then it is all the various communications that maintain life at their level, of the *qi* through the meridians, of the heart with the organs, of the organs between themselves, of the internal viscera with external parts of the body, of that which is inside the body with that which has to go outside. For example, to indicate constipation or anuria one often simply says *bu tong* (不通), no communication.

There is another character which is very interesting to compare with this one. The central portion is the same but instead of the radical for a march or circulation you have the radical for illness. You then get a character which is pronounced the same, *tong* (痛), and which means pain. This means that pain is thought of as a bad functioning and a cessation of this free communication that forms life at all levels. The relationship between these two characters is attested in all the texts. For example they say where there is no longer free communication then there is pain, and when you re-establish free communication then there is no more pain.

Claude Larre: You have the same thing with water. When water is no longer free moving then it easily becomes stagnant, and when you unblock it it becomes clear again. It is based on the same phenomenon that life being free circulation from something given from above, is received and goes further, and is communicated. Water and life are made of the same qualities. That is the reason why Lao zi chapter 8 says so much about water. Of course in life there should be water and fire, so water is not the only image for the flow of life, but it is one. We are attracted by rivers, in most major capital cities there is a river, and rivers are beneficial for the inspiration they give, showing that everything has to flow. The Chinese are very interested in flowing since they see flowing even in things that we do not. If life is flowing in them then they feel refreshed.

QUESTIONS

Question: Could we go over the characters for *jin ye* (津 液)?

Elisabeth Rochat: Both have the water radical. In *ye* (液) the phonetic part is the night. That is to say that there is a *yin* power of something that is shadowy, of the depths and darkness. This is very good to indicate the quality of these *ye* liquids which are more dense and which are attracted towards the condensation and the concentration in the internal parts of the body such as the articulations and joints, or the internal systems of the sense organs and the brain. The brain needs a considerable amount of liquid irrigation, and there is what is called the progression of these liquids towards the top in order to irrigate the brain and the internal systems of the orifices.

Jin (津) represents the other aspect of the movement of liquids, that which pushes the circulation towards the exterior, and which does not make them concentrate or stay in one place, but to circulate without stopping and finally to evacuate outside the body. It is the movement that makes the liquids circulate in all the interstices between the flesh and the skin, and their evacuation is produced in particular in the form of urine or sweat.

The pronunciation of the phonetic *jin* (津) is very close to *qing* (清) and *jing* (精). It is this character that you find in the name of the town Tianjin which lies between Beijing and the sea. In non-medical language *jin* (津) means a ford in a river, some kind of passage that is made between water and earth. In the name of Tianjin the *jin* is coupled with the character *tian* (天) meaning heaven, thereby drawing the character towards the *yang* (陽) with the possibility of diffusion and circulation.

Question: Could you say more about the phrase 'median void' which we had earlier?

Claude Larre: Everything appears and disappears. To have a place for something to appear there must be a void. The void is the highest quality in nature and is necessarily in the middle. So median void is an expression for the flux of life between heaven and earth. Because man is in the third position after heaven and earth we usually say heaven, earth and man, but if we want to locate the position of man we place him in the middle between heaven and earth. If the number three has been thought of as exemplifying *qi* (氣) it is because in the Chinese character you write a stroke on top, a smaller one in the middle and another bigger one underneath. It means that the main consideration is what is surging in between the two big lines. This flux or flow is water or fire or *qi*. *Qi* is always that which is between two, hence median void.

Question: In pre-Buddhist Chinese thought is there as much consideration given to the idea of emptiness?

Claude Larre: The Mawangdui banner is striking for the place given to the void at the top. The immortals' paradise is not seen, although the environment is minutely described. But coming down the banner we see there is an opening to heaven with two guards and a void between them. Below are two phoenixes with a flower in the middle. The void is occupied by *yin* and *yang*, with *yin* at rest and *yang* on top. It is a representation of how *yin* and *yang* may be conceived in a world which is neither the material, tangible world, nor the immortals' paradise. Underneath the flower is the dark brown coloured ball of the Yellow emperor which is similar to the void because it is round. Below this there is a big empty space with no place for anything other than servants coming from heaven and the three *hun* (魂) of the deceased people.

So the median void is not actually empty in this pre-Buddhist consideration. Moving on down the banner we see *yin* and *yang* crossing in the *bi* (璧), the disc of heaven. This void is the place where *yin* and *yang* cross, and from that place the flux of life derives. When we reach the bottom there are two dragons, and at the crossing of their bodies is another void. But this void is empty. So we have different versions of the void but the void is always there.

It is true that when we want to understand what a meridian or a point is or something like that, we have to discard all representations where too much is filled in, in order that we leave space for the flux of life to be. What is important is that something is operating somewhere, and this is beyond description. We only understand that it exists through its effects. It would be silly to say that we are not able to understand what the Chinese pretend to do with acupuncture. The question is not that we do not know what it is but that we have even less ways than the Chinese for expressing how life is proceeding. The entering of life is known and the ending of life is known and the process of life is known. It is known through these twelve *zang* which describe it perfectly. But the representation of that is very difficult in Chinese, and more difficult in our own languages. The only way is to try and know through oneself what it is to be a living person, and to understand that if we make too great a materialization of what we are talking about then we block the void space which is necessary for people. This is the reason why during this seminar we have used all sorts of means, comparison, analysis, textual study, using Chinese and Franco-English, just so that within this whirlpool people are free to think and find something inside. That is my personal conclusion!

APPENDIX

Su wen chapter 8
Text and translation

LING LAN MI DIAN LUN
靈 蘭 秘 典 論

Huang di *wen yue*
黃 帝 問 曰

yuan wen shi er zang zhi xiang shi gui jian he ru
願 聞 十 二 藏 之 相 使 貴 賤 何 如

Qi Bo dui yue
岐 伯 對 曰

xi hu zai wen ye qing sui yan zhi
悉 乎 哉 問 也 請 遂 言 之

xin zhe jun zhu zhi guan ye shen ming chu yan
心 者 君 主 之 官 也 神 明 出 焉

fei zhe xiang fu zhi guan zhi jie chu yan
肺 者 相 傅 之 官 治 節 出 焉

gan zhe jiang jun zhi guan mou lü chu yan
肝 者 將 軍 之 官 謀 慮 出 焉

dan zhe zhong zheng zhi guan jue duan chu yan.
膽 者 中 正 之 官 決 斷 出 焉

tan zhong zhe chen shi zhi guan xi le chu yan
膻 中 者 臣 使 之 官 喜 樂 出 焉

pi wei zhe cang lin zhi guan wu wei chu yan
脾 胃 者 倉 廩 之 官 五 味 出 焉

da chang zhe chuan dao zhi guan bian hua chu yan
大 腸 者 傳 道 之 官 變 化 出 焉

xiao chang zhe shou sheng zhi guan hua wu chu yan
小 腸 者 受 盛 之 官 化 物 出 焉

shen zhe zuo qiang zhi guan ji qiao chu yan
腎 者 作 強 之 官 技 巧 出 焉

san jiao zhe jue du zhi guan shui dao chu yan
三 焦 者 決 瀆 之 官 水 道 出 焉

pang guang zhe zhou du zhi guan jin ye cang yan qi hua ze neng chu yi
膀 胱 者 州 都 之 官 津 液 藏 焉 氣 化 則 能 出 矣

fan ci shi er guan zhe bu de xiang shi ye
凡 此 十 二 官 者 不 得 相 失 也

THE SECRET TREATISE OF THE SPIRITUAL ORCHID
A translation of the complete text of Su wen chapter 8

Huang di asked: I wish to be instructed on the relative charges of the twelve *zang* and their relative ranks.

Qi Bo replied: What a vast question! If you will allow me, let us go over it all.

The heart holds the office of lord and sovereign. The radiance of the spirits stems from it.

The lungs hold the office of minister and chancellor. The regulation of the life-giving network stems from it.

The liver holds the office of general of the armed forces. Assessment of circumstances and conception of plans stem from it

The gallbladder is responsible for what is just and exact. Determination and decision stem from it.

Tan zhong has the charge of resident as well as envoy. Elation and joy stem from it.

The spleen and stomach are responsible for the storehouses and granaries. The five tastes stem from them.

The large intestine is responsible for transit. The residue from transformation stems from it.

The small intestine is responsible for receiving and making things thrive. Transformed substances stem from it.

The kidneys are responsible for the creation of power. Skill and ability stem from them.

The triple heater is responsible for the opening up of passages and irrigation. The regulation of fluids stems from it.

The bladder is responsible for regions and cities. It stores the body fluids. The transformations of the *qi* then give out their power.

These twelve charges form an interdependent group that allows of no failing.

If then the sovereign radiates (virtue), those under him will be at peace. From this the nurturing of life will give longevity, from generation to generation, and the empire will radiate with a great light. But if the sovereign does not radiate (virtue), the twelve charges will be in danger, which will cause the closing and blocking of the ways, finally stopping communication and the body will be seriously injured. From this the nurturing of life will sink into disaster. Everything that lives under heaven will be threatened in its ancestral line with the greatest of dangers. Take care, I repeat, take good care!

The supreme Way is in the imperceptible, change and transformation without end! Who then would know its origin? Alas, it disappears and one searches anxiously for it! Who then would know the essential? Oh, the anguish of actual situations! Who then will know how to act properly?

Countless appearances and disappearances, out of which come forth the finest threads, fine threads that multiply until you can weigh and measure them. By the thousand and ten thousand they increase and grow, through development and growth creating the bodily form, governed by rules.

Huang di concluded: The teaching on the brilliant radiance of the essences and the conduct of the great saints has just been expounded. So to treat the declaration and elucidation of this great teaching with the respect it deserves, after purification and exorcism, an auspicious day will be chosen.

Huang di then had the fates consulted. A favourable and auspicious day was chosen, and they then proceeded to the Chamber of the Spiritual Orchid to deposit the teaching and to ensure its true transmission.

INDEX

INDEX

anger   68
Art of War   67
autumn   10, 11, 17, 93, 111, 126

bao   38, 104
Beijing   93, 147, 162
bian hua, change and transformation   117, 118, 121, 124, 69
bing, disease   16
bladder   32, 80, 83, 121, 124, 125, 126, 145, 146 - 153, 155, 171
blood   38, 44, 45, 53, 54, 62, 69, 71, 83, 100, 103, 112, 128, 129, 148
bones   133, 135, 136
Book of Odes   11
brain   40, 134, 140, 161
branches, terrestrial   64
bu tong   160

cang, store   26, 149, 151
cang, storehouse   110, 111
Chamfrault   39
chen, servant   27, 28, 60, 90, 91, 92, 96, 103
chuan, transmit   116, 117, 124
clear, *qing*   82, 83, 86, 87, 125, 131, 139
Confucianism   45

da chang, large intestine   115 - 118
dan, gallbladder   73 - 89

dao 1, 116
Dao de jing , 116
Daoism 1, 45
du, capital 147
du mai 152

ear 140, 141
earth 8, 10, 13, 23, 29, 30, 47, 53, 61, 65, 67, 74, 75, 82, 94, 96, 110, 112, 117, 118, 129, 130, 147, 155, 162
east 30, 65, 126
elements, five 19, 20, 31, 42, 64, 156
essences, *jing* 27, 30, 33, 34, 35, 43, 44, 45, 82, 86, 87, 111, 112, 113, 126, 129, 134, 135, 136, 138, 139, 141, 144, 149, 150, 151, 172
extraordinary *fu* 81, 82, 86, 87
extraordinary meridians 33, 35, 81

fei, lung 46 - 57, 59, 104, 128
fire 32, 54, 71, 80, 98, 137, 143, 144, 145, 151, 152, 160
five 14, 27, 28, 29, 30, 31, 32, 42
five tastes 12, 110, 112, 113, 114, 124, 171
Forbidden City 37, 103
four 29, 30, 31, 65, 82, 95
four seasons 10, 11, 13, 17, 30
fu, organ 28, 32, 110
fu, chancellor 51
Fuxi 53

gallbladder 73 - 89, 111, 143, 155, 158, 170
gan, liver 58 - 72
gan, stem 64
gong, palace 40
green, *qing* 65, 82, 83, 112, 126

guan, charge   22, 27, 40, 60, 62, 110
gui, ghost   48

Han dynasty   26, 106
heart   6, 22, 29, 36 - 48, 50, 51, 52, 53, 54, 62, 66, 77, 88, 92. 93, 96, 98, 100, 101, 103, 104, 135, 136, 137, 139, 140, 155, 157
heart governor   37, 39, 97
heart meridian   137
heater, lower   87, 98, 145, 151, 153
heater, middle   54, 97, 98, 100, 113, 145
heater, upper   86, 87, 98, 129, 145
heaven   3, 7, 8, 9, 11, 12, 13, 14, 15, 16, 17, 21, 22, 23, 24, 29, 30, 34, 37, 46, 47, 51, 53, 64, 67, 74, 75, 76, 82, 83, 95, 101, 108, 110, 112, 123, 139, 155, 157, 162, 163
heaven, anterior   43, 105
heaven, posterior   80, 84
hua, transmutation   117, 118, 121, 123, 124, 130, 131
Huang di   8, 26
hun   69, 86, 87, 127, 128, 129, 130, 163

ji, crossbow   85
ji, arts, techniques   134
jiang, strong   59, 66, 67
jiao, burner, heater   144
jie, knot   56
jin, muscular forces   107
jin ye, body fluids   145, 148, 156, 161, 162
jing, essence   43, 82, 83, 113, 126, 129, 138, 162
jing shen   135
jing wei   113
joy   90, 92, 96, 101, 103
jue, decision, determination   77, 78, 143

jue yin 14
jun, lord 37, 40, 52, 96, 104
jun, armed forces 59, 67

kidneys 32, 69, 70, 83, 88, 122, 132 - 141, 145, 152, 155

large intestine 83, 115 - 118, 120, 121, 122, 124, 126, 130, 139
Lao zi 1, 104, 138, 160
le, joy 92, 101, 102
Li po 83
lin, granaries 109, 111
ling lan, spiritual orchid 23
Ling shu 5, 54
liquids 44, 77, 83, 111, 125, 143, 151, 152, 155, 161, 162
liver 6, 22, 47, 58 - 72, 76, 78, 79, 87, 88, 101, 104, 111, 112, 114, 128, 129, 140
lü, reflection 61
lung 49 - 57, 63, 66, 69, 77, 88, 98, 100, 101, 104, 126, 128, 129, 131, 145
luo, connection 38, 104

mai, vital circulation 38, 100, 101, 103, 107, 116
marrow 135, 136, 140
Mawangdui 163
men, door 130
ming, destiny, mandate 108
ming men 32, 80, 98, 137, 144, 145, 151, 152
ming, radiance 157
Morant, Souilé de 39
muscular force 69, 72, 112, 152

Nanjing, city 147

Nan jing, classic   5, 106
nao gong, brain   40
nei, inner   91
Nei jing   5, 8, 30, 124, 127, 145, 154
Nei jing, ling shu   5, 54
Nei jing, su wen   6, 7, 40, 43, 65, 78, 82, 97, 103, 108, 114, 123, 133
nu, anger   68
Nügua   53

pang guang, bladder   146 - 153
pi, spleen   109 - 114, 116
po   56, 86, 88, 126, 127, 128, 130, 131, 139
po, residue   126, 127, 131

qi, ancestral, see also *zong*   97, 98, 100, 103, 105, 106, 107
qi, authentic, see also *zhen*   32, 105, 108
qi, defensive, see also *wei*   103
qi, nutritive, see also *ying*   103
qi, original, see also *yuan*   80, 81, 84, 105, 106
qi, sea of   87, 97, 98, 107
qi, extraordinary   81
qiang, fortitude   133, 134, 138
qiao, skill   134, 137
Qi Bo   8, 26, 162
qing, clear   82, 83, 162
qing, colour of life   82, 83

Ren 17   97

san jiao, triple heater   142 - 145
shao yang   14, 16, 77, 79, 80, 84, 137, 143
shao yin   14, 41, 136

shen, spirits   17, 41, 43, 46, 47, 48, 86, 88, 135
shen ming   36 43, 92, 101
shen, kidneys   122, 132 - 141
sheng, prosper   122, 123, 125
sheng, life   17, 56
shi, begin   56
shi, envoy   90, 92, 96, 103
shi er, twelve   22
shi ji, occasion   85
shou, to receive   122, 123
shui dao   142, 143
si, four   17
si, think   61
six   14, 15, 16, 19, 20, 29, 32, 64
small intestine   83, 116, 117, 119 - 131, 139
sperm   138, 139, 140
spirit(s)   14, 15, 17, 24, 30, 31, 36, 39, 41, 43, 45, 46, 47, 48, 54, 86, 96, 101, 129, 131, 135, 136, 139, 140
spleen   54, 86, 88, 109 - 114, 121, 124, 130, 145, 155
spring   6, 10, 11, 17, 22, 23, 65, 70, 79, 111, 126
stems, heavenly   64
stomach   24, 32, 54, 83, 86, 109 - 114, 120, 121, 122, 124, 130, 145, 155
summer   10, 11, 17, 70
Sun zi   67
Su wen, see Nei jing su wen

tai, embryo   55
tai cang, big storehouse   111
tai yang   14, 16, 151, 152
tai yin   14
tan zhong   59, 87, 90 - 108

Tang dynasty   83
Temple of Heaven   93, 96, 101, 137
tian, heaven   16, 17, 60, 162
tian gan, heavenly stem   64
Tianjin   162
tian tan   93, 95, 96
tian yun   9, 10
tong, communication   7, 159, 160
tong, pain   160
triple heater   50, 62, 77, 80, 121, 124, 142 - 145, 147, 151, 152, 155
twelve   22, 24, 25, 28, 29, 30, 32 - 35, 60, 64, 81, 86, 95, 153

void   45, 46, 144, 162 - 165

water   32, 80, 143 - 145, 147, 148, 152, 160
wei, stomach   109 - 114, 116
wei, taste   110, 112
wei, refined   113
wei, danger   158
will, *zhi*   32, 136
winter   10, 11, 17, 70, 93, 101, 111
wood   22, 112
wu, things   121, 123, 130, 131
wu wei, five tastes   12, 113
wu, shamaness   24

xi, joy   90, 92, 101
xi, connection   40, 41, 42, 45, 140
Xia dynasty   143
xiang, minister   51, 154
xiao   120
xiao chang, small intestine   116, 119 - 131

xin, heart   36 - 48, 104
xin bao luo   38, 97, 104
xin xi   40, 45, 140
xin zhong   41
xin zhu   37, 39, 41, 97, 103

yang ming   14, 16, 84
yi, purpose   88
yu, rain   24
yuan qi   82, 84, 105
yue, month   79
yun   60, 111

zang   21, 22, 26, 32, 51, 59, 60 - 62, 82, 86, 150
zhe   59, 62
zhen, authentic   60, 108
zhen qi   32, 105
zheng, correct   74, 79
zheng yue   79
zhi, regulate   55, 56
zhi, will   88
zhong, centre   41, 74, 91, 97, 104
Zhou dynasty   63
zhu, master   40, 52, 96, 157
Zhuang zi   1, 79
zi gong   40
zong qi   13, 97, 98, 100, 103, 105, 106
zuo, arousing   133, 138, 139